There Will Be Someone
to Follow Us

Dr. Alton E. Loveless

Copyright © 2013

by

Dr. Alton E. Loveless

All scripture verses are from the

KJV, NKJ and Living Bible Paraphrase Versions of the Bible.

This book was printed in the United States of America.

To order additional copies of this book, contact:

FWB Publications
527 Virginia Street
Ashville, Ohio 43103
alton.loveless@prodigy.net

Table of Contents

Dedication

Dr. Bradley Freeman and Dr. Ramakrishna Venkatesh
Dr. Raad Roubey, Dr. Erik Houttuin and Adam Salaber P.A.
Their abilities gave me an extension of life.

To the Lord who is the Great Physician and healer.

Randy, Melissa, Emily Jo, Zach, Jenn, Claire Marie
Steven, Tammy, Lucas, Whitney and Rachel Loveless
My sons and their families.

Glenna and Jesse Duggar
My sister and her husband.

To my wife, Ellen Delois
Whose love continues to engender our wholesome relationships.

Dr. Alton E. Loveless

Introduction

I have been a writer and publisher for many years, but writing a novel was completely a new adventure for me. It began as an idea I had while confined for 143 days in two St. Louis hospitals.

Upon returning home, I found that my wife had prepared a rehabilitation room for me equipped with a new computer and DSL connection next to my hospital bed for my entertainment. To keep from feeling sorry for myself and to help ease the discomfort I had, I began to write what I had envisioned months before.

For 40 years I had been involved in roles that brought me into contact with so many ministers and church leaders. Often many godlypeople had betrayed these ministers and caused detours in their ministries, missions, and even marriages. There was unhappiness and confusion and a desire by wives to leave the fishbowl life. Some ministers left while others feared to even enter.

I have known the heartbreak of missionaries hurt as their children were submitted to other cultures and who had difficulty because of their restrictions or inability to rejoin our American way.

I am assured that God has never made a mistake in His call. The proof comes from the hundreds of clergy, missionaries and their families that I have seen fulfilled to great satisfaction as they remained faithful and completed the decision of His will for their lives.

While the characters in this book are fictional, their struggles and successes are represented of real lives that I have been privileged to be a part of for so many years.

It reaches into so many genres: Romance, war, ministry, missions, relationship, history, and reward. It will touch your heart.

Just as I enjoyed writing this novel for my therapy, it is my hope that you will feel my love and empathy for others whose joy needs lifting.

Dr. Alton E. Loveless
Alton.loveless@prodigy.net

BAIL OUT

Thirty minutes into the reconnaissance flight over Thailand Captain Nichols radioed in with an elevated voice of fear, "Oh, man! There are fifteen MiGs at 9 o'clock and closing in on us."

"What are they doing in this area?" Colonel Glenn replied in a worried voice. Within seconds of that communication the MiGs began to open fire, and a dogfight ensued.

Colonel Joe Glenn's F-105 squadron had begun combat air patrol flights ten days after arriving at the Royal Thailand Air Force Base in Udorn, Thailand. This was their first overseas assignment following their training at Kelly Air Force Base in San Antonio, Texas and none of the young officers had been in action before.

With Colonel Glenn at the point, each man was located in the position assigned them during their training at Kelly. Lieutenant Allen "Do-Gooder" Livingston was on the left wing; Lieutenant Sam Cunningham on the right wing, Captain Jeff Nichols was positioned between the wings with Lieutenant Donald Brogan and Lieutenant Robert Grissom flying beside each other and directly behind.

"There are three MiGs buzzing all around me. I'm in a bad position," Lieutenant Grissom shouted frantically.

Colonel Glenn's command came in a firm voice, "Gentlemen, protect yourselves."

Lieutenant Livingston was the first to leave formation saying nervously, "I'll take the front plane." As he tailed the MiG and shot it down he shouted with a pounding heart, "Bingo! Bingo! Mark me down one!"

"Grissom where are you? Grissom come back!" Cunningham pled as he frantically searched the skies for sight of his partner.

"At 4 o'clock and running hard," came the breathless reply. "Come help me now. They are all over me."

"Roger" replied Cunningham as he banked his plane and maneuvered into position behind Grissom. "I see the MiG on your tail. I've got him in my sites."

Cunningham quickly took out the MiG on Grissom's tail and with excitement from his first kill shouted, "Got him! He's gone Grissom."

Livingston now on his way back to rejoin the formation saw another unprotected MiG and quickly locked his sites on the enemy. He fired off one of his wing rockets and watched the trail of fire become an explosion as the MiG remnants descended to the ground. "I can't believe it! Wow! Wow! I got another one," Livingston shouted.

With thirteen MiGs still in the air Livingston concentrated on maneuvering his plane back into formation to aid his squadron when Brogan broke the radio silence. "Livingston! There's a MiG on your backside!"

"Roger! Roger! Go get him," Livingston shouted back while preparing to take his Thunderchief into Mach speed. He headed straight up to nearly 50,000 feet, knowing the Chinese made MiG-17 could not compete with his F-105.

While circling from that altitude, Livingston could see his outnumbered squadron and the MiGs swarming like angry bees in the sky. Knowing he had to get back into the fight he assessed the positions of the MiGs as he descended. He could see that Nichols' position had left him vulnerable to enemy fire and there was a MiG crowding his left wing.

"Get that guy off my wing," cried Nichols. "Come on! Someone shoot him before he gets me," he pled louder.

"Roger!" answered Livingston in a calming voice. "I'll get him Nichols." As Livingston closed in on the MiG he whispered, "Come on Babe, just a little closer. Come on Babe. You are right where I want you."

After firing a number of rounds from his turret gun, smoke from the enemy plane revealed he had made another successful hit. Suddenly there came a flaming explosion as his third MiG lost its fight and spiraled down through the clouds.

"Bingo!" was all he said as he headed back into the midst of the battle where MiGs continued tearing up the sky.

"I'm hit!" The commanding voice of Colonel Glenn could be heard in every man's ears. "If there's any chance of saving this plane, I've gotta head back to base immediately. Stay in there men. Make me proud!"

"Do-Gooder! Do-Gooder! You've got one heading toward you at 5 o'clock," shouted Cunningham. "Fly right! Fly right! They are swarming all around us," he continued in a hoarse shout.

Hoping to lose the enemy plane, Livingston banked right to 3 o'clock and then immediately rolled left again. He continued flying this pattern while staring over his shoulder into the face of the enemy MiG. It was close enough now that he could see the pilot's helmet shining in the sun.

As he was radioing, "I can't lose him!" he felt the impact of the enemy bullets as they riddled his plane. Each bullet shook the plane and a sudden fear came over Livingston as the reality of trouble sank in to his thoughts. He had no idea how many places his plane had been hit, but his cockpit was damaged badly. His glass canopy had shattered and he was breathing the outside air. The smell of smoke brought his attention to the fact that his engine had been taken out as well.

"I'm hit! I'm hit!" he shouted frantically.

"Roger!" replied Captain Nichols. "Brogan, stay with Livingston," he commanded.

Livingston tried to pull out of the battle zone with his little remaining power as he radioed, "Brogan, I've been hit hard. My plane is nearly out of control. Watch me down."

Brogan found the plane following Livingston and in a rage began to fire all his ammunition into the tailing enemy jet. "Don't worry about the plane following you, Livingston. I got it." Livingston; however, had disappeared from his sight.

With Livingston down and the planes scattered, Captain Nichols noticed a brief retreat of the MiGs. "Gentlemen," he commanded, "Regroup and let's return to base while we've got a chance."

While the remaining squadron turned for home, Captain Nichols assessed the position and condition of each plane. "Cunningham, where are you?" he called.

"I headed home moments ago," was the weak reply.

The New Land

Lieutenant Allen Livingston's plane was helpless and shook uncontrollably as it spiraled downward. Losing the fight to save his plane, Livingston engaged the ejection button with only moments to spare. As he watched his abandoned plane breaking up just a few hundred feet away he became aware of an intense pain in his right calf. With a quick glance he saw blood flowing from a bullet wound. As his plane crashed in a ball of fire, he himself hit the ground and passed out after bouncing several times.

The noise of the explosions and firing of guns had caught the attention of several men working at a nearby compound. The men watched as Allen's parachute opened, and they ran toward the place they thought it would land.

It took several minutes for the men to climb the steep and rocky terrain, but they managed to find Allen lying in a heap among the briers and forest growth. Their initial observation found Allen unconscious and losing a lot of blood. Cutting away Allen's right pants' leg revealed the source of the bleeding and one of the young men, Ling Kai, a nurse's aide from the compound's clinic, immediately tore a strip from his shirt and tied it around the wound to stop the blood flow. As the aide tended to Allen, the other two men began to fashion a stretcher out of two young tree limbs and some thick vines.

The jostling of moving Allen from his ensnared parachute and onto the stretcher woke him. Moaning with pain the three men realized he was in shock. The aide began talking to him in soothing tones to try and reassure him that they would get him help as quickly as possible. Using what was left of the parachute the three young men wrapped Allen tight and began the long and dangerous trip back down the rocky bluff and through the thick undergrowth.

It had taken several hours after finding Allen to prepare him and get him carried back to the compound where he was immediately taken to the medical clinic.

Dr. Malin Rasmussen, founder of the clinic, began checking Allen's vital signs as Ling removed Allen's bloodied pants. Dr. Rasmussen checked the deep wound on Allen's right leg and noticed the large amount of lost blood.

"Ling, get Dr. Angelika. This man is going to need a blood transfusion and immediate surgery," Dr. Rasmussen ordered while searching out the soldier's dog tags. Upon finding the tags he called, "And check our donor list for anyone with O+ blood." As Dr. Rasmussen continued his survey of Allen's wounds he muttered, "Stuck out here in the middle of nowhere with no blood bank for miles. How are we supposed to save this airman if we can't find enough blood?"

"We are going to pray for the Lord to provide," came the calm reply from Dr. Angelika, Malin's wife and co-founder of the clinic. She quickly joined her husband in assessing the soldier's needs.

Dr. Rasmussen noticed Angelika's lips moving in prayer and he couldn't help but notice the look of peace she wore. He wondered to himself why he couldn't grasp that same faith in God. Why did he always feel like he was the only one who could control the emergencies? He was trying to reason this in his mind when Ling burst back into the room with his arms full of the items Dr. Angelika had requested for him to bring in preparation for the transfusion. As he began laying them out on the table, he turned to the doctors and announced, "I, too, have O+ blood. I'll be the donor for this soldier."

Dr. Rasmussen stood looking in awe at his aide, while his wife gently touched his arm. With a knowing smile she simply stated, "Let's get scrubbed."

After several hours of surgery on Allen's leg and several pints of blood the Rasmussen's had both Allen and Ling resting comfortably. Ling, upon rising, sought Dr. Rasmussen's presence in order to discuss some thoughts that had weighed on his mind while he rested.

"I noticed that Lieutenant Livingston was carrying a small Bible in his chest pocket. I believe that he must be a fellow brother in Christ, and I would like your permission to care for him while he is here."

Dr. Rasmussen smiled at the hardworking, young man he was so fond of. "I'm sure that Lieutenant Livingston will be more than honored to have you take care of his needs. You have done such a good job of it to this point, there is no doubt that you won't continue to take excellent care of him."

Ling was so excited. He had not had the opportunity to befriend many Christian men since seeking refuge in the compound three years ago, and he knew that he would have an opportunity to practice the English that he had studied during high school.

For three days Ling tended the unconscious Lieutenant. It was early one morning as the light began to shine on Allen's face that Ling heard his weak voice ask for a drink. Ling immediately went for a glass of cool water and let Dr. Rasmussen know their patient was awake.

As Ling braced Allen's shoulders and helped him sip the water Dr. Rasmussen entered the small room. "Hello, young man. It's nice to see you awake this morning. I'm Dr. Malin Rasmussen and this young man is Ling Kai. He and his brothers found you and saved your life."

Allen was surprised to learn that this man speaking was his doctor. The man was very muscular and obviously kept himself in excellent condition. Most of the doctors Allen was familiar with were generally small, slender, and not athletically built gentlemen. Allen was even more surprised at the doctor's clear, distinct English.

"Where am I?" he managed to ask.

"You are at a medical clinic in rural Laos," came the sympathetic reply. Laos? The word echoed in Allen's mind as he drifted to sleep once again. As the thought assailed his unconscious mind, his sleep became fitful. By that afternoon he developed a high fever and kept calling out, "You cost $14."

Ling did his best to keep the young lieutenant comfortable, and for another two days kept a nursing vigil by his side. Finally the fever broke and Allen woke drenched with perspiration. Ling called for his brothers to help change the bedding and make the lieutenant more comfortable again.

As the three young men worked, Dr. Rasmussen returned to check Allen's vital signs. Before they left the room, Dr. Rasmussen introduced them to Allen. "You have met Ling. These other two men are his brothers Lang and Noi. They live here in the compound. Five days ago they were working outside the walls when they heard the machine gun sounds of the aerial fight. They saw your plane going down, and when they noticed your parachute they were able to follow your descent and found you entangled in some brush out on the mountain side. They rescued you and made sure you were not seen by any enemy."

The three Chinese boys were not very large. Ling was the tallest and oldest. He was about five feet eight inches tall. Lang was an inch or so shorter and a little on the heavy side. Noi, at the young age of ten, was much smaller still.

Allen pondered to himself how these boys could have managed getting him to the clinic. He was only one hundred and sixty pounds, but they seemed so small and young. "Thank you," he managed to whisper.

As the boys humbly left, Dr. Rasmussen began his examination of Allen's leg. "You lost a lot of blood, Lieutenant. Ling, here, willingly gave his blood for your transfusion. It took Dr. Angelika and me several hours to get that leg pieced back together. You should be able to walk again after some rehabilitation, but it's not going to be an easy road. You will have to stay completely off it for at least six weeks. Since your fever is now gone, all your vital signs are back to normal. How about a light meal?"

With a brief thought, Allen weakly replied, "I think I could handle that." As Ling left to get Allen's meal, Dr. Rasmussen moved a chair next to the bed and studied Allen. "You are Lieutenant Allen Livingston?" He questioned.

"Yes sir, I am."

"And you are an American?"

"Yes sir, I am."

"I know, with the condition of your leg, that you are not mobile yet, but I would advise you to stay confined to this room until the news of your crashing has died down. My wife, Dr. Angelika, and I came here 30 years ago to start this compound with medical clinic and training center for the poor and displaced people in this area of Laos. The whole area is somewhat divided right now, but I don't think you are in any danger. We have had many people come in and out of our facilities, and we have continued to do so without interference. However, we need to make sure you are kept safe," concluded Dr. Rasmussen as Ling settled a small tray before Allen. "Some time when you are stronger I will tell you more about this land, the people, and our desire to come to this small, troubled country."

After the doctor left the room, Ling sat down and picked up his portion of the story. "My brothers and I have been very safe here. We escaped three years ago from our home in China. There were many persecutions against Christians who worshipped in underground or unregistered churches. We witnessed many attacks on members of our church and on our last day there we watched our godly parents beaten and murdered. We hid in an empty freight car not knowing it was going to Hanoi, Vietnam. We got off without being seen and headed west toward Laos since Northern Vietnam was under attack from various armies. After days of searching for safety farther west, a fisherman let us ride to the other side of the Mekong into Laos. We finally came upon some men in the mountains who were using elephants to pull timber from the forest. They shared lunch with us and directed us to this compound. We found our new home here."

Ling would have liked to have started a real conversation now that Allen was finished eating, but he could see that the lieutenant was growing tired again. "You need more rest now," he commented while adjusting Allen's pillows and making him comfortable once again. "I will be right here close if you need something."

"Thank you," was the soft reply as sleep once again claimed Allen.

᠁᠁᠁ ᥍᥍᥍ ᠁᠁᠁

After several days of healing sleep and light meals, Allen was gaining much strength. Ling, who hardly left his side, knew he was spending more time awake now and asked permission to question Allen.

"I will answer what I can," Allen offered.

"While you were unconscious, you kept saying something that didn't make sense to me. Over and over you would say, 'You cost $14.' Could you explain that?" asked Ling.

With a sudden faraway look on his face, Allen grinned to Ling. "Yes, I can answer that, Ling. I remember how shocked I was to find out I was in Laos right before falling unconscious again. I guess that is what triggered such thoughts of my home. That $14 comes from my day of birth.

"You see, my mother was the seventh daughter of twelve girls born to her parents in central Arkansas. That's in the central part of the United States."

"I have studied America's geography. I remember where it is," Ling answered.

"Well, if a man married one of the girls, the new husband had to raise crops for her parents for two years to pay them for her. I was born near the end of the second year in an old log house provided for my parents by my grandfather. I once asked an aunt if she had a photo of this old house that was built about 1850 according to my mother. To my amazement, she did. When I received the photo I took it to my mother and showed it to her with the query, 'Do you know whose house this is?'

"To my question she chimed back, 'That's the house you were born in! It was a Tuesday night about 7:30. There was an electrical storm with plenty of lightning and thunder,' she started. She continued by telling me all the people who were there. Then she proceeded with the story. 'The country doctor got stuck on the old dirt road, and you had to be delivered by one of the ladies in attendance before he arrived.'

"To which I said, 'So you didn't have to pay the doctor?'

'Oh, yes!' she replied. 'You still cost us $14.'

Ling chuckled at the mother's reply. He could envision his own loving mother telling such a story. Both young men looked at each other with a bonding knowledge of what they had both lost so young in life. Ling knew he would never see his mother again, and he wondered if Allen would ever make it home to his.

Breaking the silence, Allen continued, "Well, life has had many changes and the cost of everything is far above those humble days in my early life.

"In fact, just after my birth we moved to a neighboring community where my family was provided a house by the shop owner to live in, an allotment of groceries, and fifty cents a week. My dad worked as a blacksmith at a farm store and blacksmith shop repairing equipment to help the farmers get in their crops. This occurred during the War when not many new things were being built. Old machinery had to be repaired and parts made on site. My dad was kept busy.

"I remember the end of World War II a few years later. My father bought an old commando jeep and turned it into a wrecker that was used to expand his new garage and service station business.

"Our first house was in my hometown of Conway, Arkansas, and the monthly payment was $23. Dad's business grew and so did the price of everything. I don't suppose babies cost just $14 anymore," Allen concluded. He didn't voice his next thought, but lay contemplating how much more it was going to cost him to get safely home.

Ling, sensing Allen's need for time alone, got up to leave. "I thank you for sharing so much with me. I don't understand all you are telling me, but American history was my favorite class in school, and I would like to know more about your culture and people. Perhaps later you can tell me more about your growing up."

"Sure," was Allen's reply.

"You must rest now, Lieutenant," Ling suggested as he turned to go.

Allen stopped him. "Ling," he said while offering his hand. "Please just call me Allen."

Ling gripped Allen's hand, and the two knew a friendship had been born. Little did either of them know that total love and loyalty would soon develop from this relationship between Christian brothers.

About-Face

Two hours after the unexpected air strike, the four pilots finally made their return to Udorn's Royal Thailand Air Force Base. The voice from the tower radioed an inquiry to the absence of their sixth plane.

"We lost one somewhere over Laos," was the concerned reply of Captain Nichols.

After changing from their flight suits, the five pilots made their way to the debriefing room. Each man was deep in thought about his experience with the enemy and the loss of one of their own. The corridor quietly echoed their footsteps, and they were shocked by the volume of Lieutenant Cunningham's voice when they entered the room to meet Colonel Glenn and Brigadier General Rupert Masterson.

"That Do-Gooder deserted our squadron and left us all without a solid defense," he shouted to Colonel Glenn. "The coward . . ."

"That's enough," Colonel Glenn quietly warned. "We will all have an opportunity to make our statements."

It had been clear to everyone from the beginning that Lieutenant Sam Cunningham didn't like Lieutenant Livingston. Cunningham was quick to let it be known that he disliked Christian "do-gooders" and he called them all cowards. He was jealous of Livingston's camaraderie with the other squad members and superiors, and he felt no remorse for what he was planning in his mind. In order to get the heat off himself for his early departure from the fight, Cunningham once again took a stand and all but shouted, "Livingston is a traitor!"

"One more word and you will be dismissed," Colonel Glenn commanded. "Take a seat."

As all the men took their seats the tension in the air seemed to mount. Colonel Glenn simply stated, "Since I was part of the fight today, Brigadier General Masterson will be witnessing all accounts for the report. I have currently informed him of the attack upon our squadron and the events as I saw them up till my departure. Captain Nichols, I would like for you to begin."

As Captain Nichols filled the Colonel and Brigadier General in on the second half of the battle, each man in turn agreed with the Captain's assessment and added his own information regarding his actions and positions.

"Right before the MiGs began their retreat, Lieutenant Livingston radioed that he had been hit. I commanded Lieutenant Brogan to stay with Livingston. In the heat of the battle there were times when I didn't even know where everyone was. I lost sight of both Brogan and Livingston. As soon as the MiGs began their retreat, I called everyone back to formation and headed home. It was upon my final assessments that I knew Livingston and Cunningham were not with us. I never gained radio contact with Livingston, and Cunningham informed me that he was already on his way back to base."

"I had to head back to base after that Holy Joe flew away leaving me stranded. He wouldn't stay in his position. We couldn't afford to lose another plane due to that traitor," Cunningham interjected.

"Colonel," Lieutenant Grissom calmly began. "You know the battle was unexpected. It was our first encounter with an enemy. Many of us were afraid and probably all of us were out of formation at times."

"I'm sorry, Colonel," said Lieutenant Brogan joining the conversation, "but I cannot agree with Cunningham. Livingston's plane was shot up and smoking. The last words I faintly heard from him were, 'I'm hit! I'm hit!' I couldn't make out the rest of what he was saying, and then I heard Captain Nichols tell me to follow him. I took out the MiG that had been following Livingston and tried to find him, but he had disappeared," finished Brogan.

Cunningham immediately jumped back into the conversation, "He disappeared because he flew away. I'm telling you that I saw him heading out in the same direction those MiGs were retreating in.

Lieutenant Allen Livingston is a traitor."

"Young man," interrupted the Brigadier General's deep voice. "You are making a very serious accusation about one of our own. You better be absolutely sure of the details before giving any further information."

"Sir," answered Cunningham, "I am aware of what this accusation means to our squadron and Lieutenant Livingston, but I can only give you the details as they happened."

"And you want to call Lieutenant Livingston a 'traitor' in this formal report?" asked Brigadier General Masterson.

"Yes Sir, I'm afraid that is what I must do."

"Very well, Lieutenant. The report will stand, but there will be no judgment made until the rest of the investigation is completed. We must do a search for the missing plane of Lieutenant Livingston. Gentlemen, on behalf of the United States, I want to thank you for your service today." Brigadier General Masterson stood and dismissed the men.

⚓

Lieutenant Grissom went to Cunningham's room the next afternoon. Finding him calmed down from the day before Grissom began, "I never thanked you for taking out the MiG on my tail. I appreciate your help in keeping me in the air."

The MiG had been Cunningham's first kill, and he had taken several opportunities around the base to brag about his shot. Grissom knew that his visit would inflate Cunningham's ego, but he wanted to break the ice between the two of them. He knew the tension in their squadron was going to have to ease if they were going to fly efficiently together in their upcoming assignments.

The squadron continued to fly in Southeast Asia and participated in many major strikes in North Vietnam. They won the Air Force Cross for their participation in the raid to bring down the Domer Bridge and prevent the moving of enemy ground forces.

With each success, the pilots' camaraderie grew and it seemed Cunningham's irritation against Christians was eliminated since Livingston was gone.

On one occasion, Grissom, Cunningham, and the others were sitting in the mess hall when Brogan suddenly announced, "I really miss Livingston being here. I would have thought that we would have heard something about him by now."

Cunningham said, "You know, I didn't think I would ever miss him until he was gone. Now I don't have anyone to argue with."

The others agreed and began to reminisce about Livingston and share their theories as to how the investigation was progressing. Then one by one they began to leave the hall. When Grissom and Cunningham were the only two left, Grissom eyed Cunningham directly and asked, "Would there be a change in our friendship if I told you I was a Christian?"

Startled, Cunningham replied, "No! Not you!"

With a grin Grissom answered, "Yes, me."

"Well, you are different than most Christians I knew back home in Oklahoma," Cunningham said in a somewhat subdued fashion.

"My father was a minister back in Missouri and one of the finest men I ever knew. He was fair, honest, and lived by the Holy Book," Grissom acknowledged. "I joined the Air Force to help my mother and sister. They have so little to live on. Every night I read my Bible and pray for them and others. I have even prayed for you."

"You're a preacher's kid? I can't believe it." Cunningham paused and shifted briefly in his seat. "Would you believe that I'm a preacher's kid too?"

"I think I hear an all too familiar story coming," lamented Grissom.

"What do you mean?"

"I mean, it always seems that something happens in the lives of preachers' kids that make them run away from Christianity," answered Grissom.

"You are right about that. My father was a good man also. In fact, he was my hero, and we did many things together. He lived for his church and for his family.

"One day, from out of the blue, someone in the church brought up some nasty charges against my father. He was greatly hurt. The deacons and leaders told my dad they didn't believe the charges, but for the well-being of the church they asked my father to resign. This broke my father and disillusioned him with the people who would not stand up for him. I couldn't understand their cowardice for not standing with my father, so the mistrust of Christians carried over to me.

"My mother was deeply hurt because of the way their former friends had treated her husband. She was a godly woman, but the hurt became bitterness, and she fell ill. Her stress caused her to have a heart attack, and she died soon after.

"My sister, who had been faithful, ran off with someone in the church and messed up her life.

"My father had to get a job to provide for his remaining family. Having only been trained in the seminary, it was difficult for him to find work. He had come straight out of the seminary and taken the church. It was his first and only. He rejoiced for months over the goodness of the Lord for that church, but then the devil took it over.

"I began to think about joining the Air Force to get away from all the hurt, especially after my dad began to drink to ease his mind. On one of his drinking nights, he ran a red light and was hit by an oncoming truck and trailer. He was killed instantly.

"Many of the former church family came to the funeral, and most told me they were very sorry. I could only sit there with my head low, becoming increasingly bitter with each remark. My hatred for that church grew, so I decided it would be best for me to enlist.

"So, Grissom, I guess that's a lot to take in about me, but maybe now you will understand me more."

"I certainly do understand now that I know more about your upbringing," replied Grissom, "But now I wish you would have known the background of Allen Livingston. He had studied for the ministry just like our fathers, but detoured because of someone he deeply loved. You see, he joined the Air Force because he was running from someone who had hurt him also. She, like your sister, got with the wrong crowd and was killed. However, unlike you, he did not neglect reading his Bible and praying. But, that's another story and another day. We better call it a night. Drills come early in the mornings."

A New Light Began

In the weeks following Cunningham's confession, he and Grissom spent more time together talking about their pasts. Lieutenant Brogan, also a fellow Christian, joined them on many of their late night talks.

Since Udorn, Thailand didn't have any Christian churches, the Lieutenants Brogan and Grissom had been attending chapel on the base. Their newest chaplain reminded them of Reverend Bob Graham, their chaplain back at Kelly. Both men were very interesting and ministered from their hearts. The lieutenants were always eager to attend every available service.

One Sunday morning Cunningham met them on their way to service and asked where they were headed.

In unison they answered, "To chapel."

"Would you mind if I joined you?"

"No sir!" Brogan began, "You are certainly welcomed. You'll like this guy."

They arrived at the small chapel where fifteen others were already gathered for the service. While Brogan and Grissom chose seats, Cunningham took in the scarce surroundings. This was the first time he had stepped foot in a church since his father's funeral, and he was somewhat taken aback by the plainness of the chapel.

The church he had grown up in was always so warm and welcoming. Cunningham could vividly remember the warm shades of blue, the beautiful stained glass windows, and the wooden pulpit where his father preached. He could see the large picture of Jesus looking over the congregation, and he remembered the comfortably padded pews that while in childhood he so often fell asleep on or played under. He could see the flowers that surrounded the altar where he so often knelt to be with the Lord.

The memories brought a pain of regret to Cunningham, but he realized the cold barrenness of the military chapel mirrored the coldness he now felt in his own heart. As the songster began to lead the small congregation in the old hymn "Just as I Am," Cunningham joined his friends in the row of cold metal chairs. The words of the old hymn that Cunningham remembered so well began to resonate in his soul, and he looked quickly around the small chapel, debating whether he should walk out or stay.

As the song ended, the songster asked for another suggested hymn from the congregation. Grissom, sensing the unrest in his friend, lightly touched Cunningham's arm and gave him a smile of encouragement.

"How about 'When the Roll is Called Up Yonder'," suggested Brogan.

Cunningham shrunk even further into his misery as the words of this hymn were all too familiar also. He could hear his father's deep voice preaching about the glories of Heaven, but he knew that in the condition he had let his heart become he would not be there when the roll was called. Cunningham hadn't let himself think about his soul for years, but as he sat for the preaching to begin, he found himself lost in thoughts of his current sins and situation.

As the chaplain approached the small stand he used as a pulpit, he scanned the small chapel. "I see many new faces this morning," he began. "Let me welcome you to service. I am Chaplain Andy Raines from Tulsa, Oklahoma. My message today is entitled 'It is Your Decision'."

His Midwestern drawl burst loudly with his introduction.

"Let me give you one short verse from the Holy Book that is long in substance."

"For as he thinks in his heart, so is he, from Proverbs 23:7."

"No power on Earth, or under Earth, can make a man do wrong without his consent."

The chaplain, being from Cunningham's home state, had gotten his attention. The brief introduction hit Cunningham with such force. The chaplain's voice and demeanor were so much like his father's, and Cunningham found himself listening intently to what this preacher had to say.

"In St. Louis, Missouri, there is a railroad switchyard," continued Chaplain Raines.

"One particular switch there begins with just the thinnest piece of steel to direct a train away from one main track to another. However, if you were to follow those two tracks you would find that one ends in San Francisco and the other in New York; two very different destinations, all because of one tiny switch in a switchyard in the middle of the country! Here is where God's Word comes in. The Word directs us to a very different destination than this world offers, but we can't stay on the right track unless we make the choice to switch to the track from this world to eternity. What's your destination?"

As Cunningham sat considering those words he lost track of the chaplain's message. When he could regain his focus the chaplain was saying, "The teachings of Christ reveal Him to be a realist in the finest meaning of the word. Nowhere in the Gospels do we find anything visionary or overly optimistic. He told His hearers the whole truth and let them make up their minds. He might grieve over the retreating form of an inquirer who could not face up to the truth, but He never ran after him to try to win him with rosy promises. He would have men follow Him, knowing the cost, or He would let them go their way."

As Cunningham sat there thinking the chaplain couldn't possibly affect hit any further, the conclusion managed to his him even harder still.

"Let me leave you with this thought. Max Jukes lived in New York. He did not believe in Christ or in Christian training. He refused to take his children to church, even when they asked to go. He had

1,026 descendants; 300 were sent to prison for an average term of thirteen years; 190 were public prostitutes; and 680 were admitted alcoholics. His family, thus far, has cost the state in excess of $420,000. They made no contribution to society.

"Reverend Jonathan Edwards lived in the same state at the same time as Jukes. He loved the Lord and saw that his children were in church every Sunday, and he served the Lord to the best of his ability. He had 929 descendants; 430 were ministers; 86 became university professors; 13 became university presidents; 75 authored books; and 7 were elected to the United States Congress; and one was vice president of his nation. Edwards' family never cost the state one cent, but has contributed immeasurably to the life of plenty in their day."

Cunningham thought about those statistics through the dismissal prayer and hoped it was not too late for him to change his ways for the family he hoped to have in the future.

As the three airmen walked quietly back from the chapel, Grissom and Brogan could tell Cunningham was lost in deep thought. Hoping to get Cunningham to share his burden, Brogan asked "What did you think of the service?"

"Boy! He knew how to get your attention," Cunningham sheepishly answered. Then offering no more conversation he broke away from the group and headed to a secluded area on the base.

The next few months were busy for the squadron, but the relationship between Cunningham, Grissom, and Brogan continued to grow. They continued to go to chapel whenever their busy schedule would allow, but Cunningham always kept to himself and never shared any of his more personal convictions with his friends. Grissom and Brogan, in spite of the lack of information shared by Cunningham, could see changes taking place in his life, and they continued to pray for him on a daily basis.

The Truth Is Revealed

It was quite a surprise to the squadron when they were called to meet Colonel Glenn in a debriefing room early one morning. Upon entering the room, the men found both the colonel and Brigadier General Masterson seated at the head of the table. Standing in a corner staring out the window was Captain Nichols. All three men were sober and the lieutenants knew whatever they were about to find out must be serious.

"Gentlemen," began Colonel Glenn. "We have two pieces of information to share with you today. This first part has no connection to the second. Our squadron has been very successful here in Udorn, but the fighting in this region is ending. Captain Nichols and I have both decided that this is our last assignment and we will be retiring after reporting back to Washington at the end of the week."

"This week?" questioned Brogan. "Sir, where does that leave us?"

"Your new assignments have been posted and will take affect as of tomorrow morning. You and Lieutenant Grissom have been assigned to Edwards Air Force base in California. Lieutenant Cunningham will remain in Thailand, but transferred to the base at Koret. They are in need of a right wing man, and they know that Cunningham is one of the best."

Although proud to be called one of the best, Cunningham was visibly upset over the squadron being disbanded. "Colonel, isn't there any way to keep us together?" questioned Grissom.

"No, Grissom. It appears as if our presence here is no longer needed.

There are lots of squadrons being disbanded, and since Captain Nichols and I are retiring, the Air Force felt our squad was one that could easily be transferred. And if there are no more questions regarding that, I turn to the Brigadier General for the second piece of information."

Trying to let the first bit of information still sink in, Brigadier General Masterson took the Lieutenants' silence as his consent to continue.

"Gentlemen, as we stand here today talking about disbanding our squadron, we need to remember that we have not been complete since losing Lieutenant Allen Livingston. It has been nearly a year, but the investigations are all complete and the reports have been finalized. The wreckage of Livingston's plane was never located. In all appearances he vanished. In consideration with those findings was the written testimony of Lieutenant Cunningham. The final report is that Lieutenant Allen Livingston has been found to be a traitor to the United States of America and will be accordingly dealt with should he ever be found."

"What?" shouted Grissom. "Sir, how could that be? Livingston would never have left the United States. That's not the kind of man he is."

"Surely, Sir, there has been some sort of mistake. Something that was missed in the investigation," added Brogan.

"Why didn't they just call him MIA?" pressed Grissom.

"Gentlemen," interrupted Brigadier General Masterson, "The United States doesn't pass out verdicts of 'traitor' lightly. They have done a thorough investigation, and there is nothing further that can be done."

"It wasn't easy for me to accept either, but we have no choice." These were the first words Captain Nichols had spoken. "The sooner you come to terms with it, the easier your next assignments will be."

Rising from his chair, Colonel Glenn eyed each man. "I realize you need time to think about what we have told you, but you need to be prepared to leave at first light. Take the next few hours to pack up your personal belongings. Lieutenants Grissom and Brogan, you need to lock down your planes. Lieutenant Cunningham, you will be flying yours to Koret. We will meet again directly after lunch to finish putting the details into place."

As the three airmen left the meeting room, Grissom and Brogan couldn't help but notice how silent Cunningham had been and the look of horror that he still wore.

"Hey, Cunningham, are you all right?" questioned Grissom.

Cunningham, having retreated into silence, kept walking with no response. Grissom looked at Brogan and the two just shrugged. They all three headed for their rooms to begin cleanup.

The afternoon went quickly for the squadron as they finalized their tour in Udorn, Thailand. Grissom and Brogan had plans to spend that evening with Cunningham, but Cunningham was nowhere to be found.

"I wouldn't have thought that Cunningham would have taken the news about Livingston so roughly," suggested Brogan.

"He's been changing so much these past couple of weeks. He keeps to himself so much more now. I'm finding it hard to carry a conversation with him at all anymore," added Grissom.

Up early the next morning, Lieutenants Grissom and Brogan tried to talk with Cunningham, but their conversation contained only the formalities of saying goodbye. Cunningham was the first to go. He saluted Colonel Glenn and Captain Nichols with wishes of luck for the future. He shook hands with his friends, and while he would have liked to have poured his heart out to them, he knew that was not a possibility. Calling Allen Livingston a traitor was one sin that could never be forgiven, and he knew he was going to have to live with it for the rest of his life. He climbed into his plane and, as he began throttling, offered a final salute to the squadron he had come to know as family. Lieutenants Grissom and Brogan had the same farewell salutes before boarding their plane for California and their new assignment.

For several months the three lieutenants were able to keep in touch with brief telegrams and a couple letters that made it through. Grissom and Brogan knew that Cunningham was still involved in the action in Thailand, so when their telegrams were no longer being answered, they were concerned for the life of their friend.

After seven weeks of hearing nothing from Cunningham, they received a telegram from Cunningham's hospital chaplain. Cunningham had managed to save his plane and return to Koret after being shot up badly, but he died shortly after. The telegram continued to explain that just before he died he told the chaplain that he had lied about Lieutenant Allen Livingston and that as a re-born Christian he did not want to be known as a coward. He further asked the chaplain to please find his former squadron mates Grissom and Brogan and tell them he had found the right switch. It was stated that Cunningham's last words were, "They will know what I mean. They will understand. Please tell them I am sorry for any grief I caused."

Brogan looked at Grissom in confusion, "The right switch?"

"Remember Chaplain Raines talking about the switchyard in St. Louis? That sermon must have been the turning point in Cunningham's life," commented Grissom.

Grissom and Brogan both dropped their heads and cried for the two friends they had lost.

"Praise the Lord. He found the right switch," Brogan breathed deeply. He was sorry to have lost Cunningham, but the news that Livingston was lost in enemy territory, if he survived the crash, took over his thoughts.

Angelika's Dream

Long before the mission where Allen crashed was established, the Lord was working in the life of the young lady who would dream big enough and have faith enough to go to Asia to help the sick and displaced people.

Angelika Mowrer was the eldest of three daughters from a wealthy family in Salzburg, Austria. Mr. Mowrer was a merchant and had many stores with an extensive business. He was known for his honesty and fairness and had gained the respect of most of the city and even his competition.

Mrs. Mowrer did not work, but was very involved in the social affairs of the city. She was well liked by the ladies whose husbands were in authority in Salzburg.

The Mowrer family's belief and faith were always strong and created a firm dedication in Angelika. She was aware that her city of Salzburg had not always been a friend to Protestants. In the winter of 1731, an Edict of Expulsion had declared that all Protestants would recant their beliefs or be banished. Now, almost 200 years later, it was apparent that the religious community had settled their differences, but there was still a low number of Protestants in the city.

Angelika was the only Protestant in her class at the parochial school, but aside from a few jealous girls, she was very popular with everyone. She was near the top of her class academically, and being very pretty, was pursued by most of the boys.

Angelika showed so much promise in her history and music lessons that her parents nurtured her in both. Her family had a plan for her life, but God had spoken to Angelika at a young age about the calling He had for her. She became very interested in being a missionary and read many books about great missionaries that God had honored. Among the most influential missionaries were David Livingstone and Jonathan Goforth.

Like Angelika, David Livingstone, as a child, dreamed of becoming a medical missionary to China to spread the Word. When he was twenty-three years old he began medical classes at the AndersonCollege in Glasgow. When he was far enough advanced in his studies of medicine and theology, he applied to the London Missionary Society for service in China.

Angelika read about Livingstone's detours and was intrigued by how the Lord worked in his life. She was saddened when she discovered that he was about to go to China when war broke out there, and he was unable to go. She was equally gladdened to learn that the Lord sent an African missionary, Robert Moffat, into his life. Robert convinced Livingstone to go to Africa with him, and she was thrilled at how his life developed as he spent many months in training, and how he was blessed in marriage to Robert's daughter, Mary.

Angelika became aware that one had to have a broad area of training to be effective. Livingston, in addition to his usual missionary work, studied the geology and natural history of the surrounding countryside. Her views on human suffering were greatly influenced by Livingstone's book *Missionary Travels*. Angelika began to immerse herself in as many books about the geology, history, and people of Southeast Asia that she could find. She found that she was continually drawn to the people in that area, and even while she was young, began to commit herself to a daily prayer time for them.

One area of the mission field began to trouble Angelika. Having been raised in a family of means, she found it hard to relate to the poor. She was grateful when she came across the book *By My Spirit* by Jonathan Goforth. In that book she found how God took him from hardship to blessings.

As she continued reading about Goforth she saw how he became incredibly involved in his church, teaching a Sunday school class and handing out tracts at the door, but was still unsatisfied. She, too, had felt unsatisfied with what she could do in her home church, but was often limited by her youth.

Angelika's desire continued to grow however, and as she neared her high school graduation she was concerned with how to tell her parents and with what her friends might think of her. Once again she drew on the life and perseverance of Goforth. In college he had been cruelly ridiculed and rejected because he was a poor farm boy. Goforth's classmates soon grew to respect him as a young man on fire for the Lord. They admired Jonathan's passion and determination for missions. Angelika prayed that she would be able to earn as much respect by her family and friends as well as those she would soon minister too.

Livingstone, Goforth, and life accounts of other missionaries gave her such awareness about the calling God had given her. She realized that life was not always pleasant for missionaries, and she read about what might happen should she fulfill the Lord's plan for her. Although she had some concerns, she also learned during her studies how faithful God was to protect and provide for His servants. It was during that time she began to develop a more dedicated trust in Him.

Angelika also noted that in addition to trusting the Lord, the missionaries she had studied each had a helpmate to share their triumphs and hardships with. She, while always dreaming of becoming a medical missionary, had also dreamed of being a wife and mother. She knew no one at the time with which she might share all her dreams, but she prayed the Lord would provide her with a loving, supporting helpmate.

Angelika soon decided to confide in her pastor, the Rev. Helmut Lathum. She told him of the calling she felt and of all the missionaries she had been studying.

"I want to do what God has asked, but what about my being a female in a foreign land?" questioned Angelika. "How do you really think it will be for me in the mission field?"

"I think it will be a struggle, but completely possible. With all the missionaries you have studied, Angelika, don't tell me you haven't read about an American named Charlotte Digges Moon?"

"No, Pastor Lathum, I haven't. She was obviously a successful missionary?"

"Yes. A very spirited and outspoken young lady; she was all of 4 feet 3 inches and affectionately known as 'Lottie.' She and her sister, Orianna, were missionaries in North China. Orianna had become a physician and proved a woman could perform as well as a man in medicine."

"I really want to follow the Lord's calling, Pastor," concluded Angelika.

"You and I both know that God's plan for our lives is the best life we could live," counseled Pastor Lathum.

Angelika knew that Pastor Lathum's words were correct, but she continued to keep her dreams private for fear others would not understand and would become dream killers.

Her Family Concern

Angelika's parents were very dear to her, and she was concerned about disappointing them with her future plans. Salzburg had three universities, and her family could afford any type education she wanted. Due to the influence of Mozart in their town, they wanted Angelika to train in music since she was already a very good pianist. Angelika, however, had her other plans and knew she was soon going to have to share them with her parents.

First, she approached her father, and after revealing many of the things she had kept hidden, she said, "Father, you and I have always been so close, and I would never want to hurt you, but I feel God wants me to do something special for Him. I am sure I am doing what He desires with a future study in medicine."

"My darling girl, I have felt for quite some time you were not just an ordinary child. I knew God was going to use you somewhere far from here. As your father I didn't want this, but I have prayed that I might have strength and peace when the time came."

"You have given me your permission to do God's will haven't you?"

"Yes," her father answered sadly, "I have."

With a hug that contained many emotions, Angelika whispered, "Thanks, Daddy."

She knew getting her mother to understand would be harder, and Angelika waited for just the right time to discuss it. The occasion came one afternoon as the two were sitting at the table for tea.

"Mother, I have something I need to talk to you about."

"Yes dear. What do you want to tell me?"

Angelika wasted no time as she blurted, "I'm going to college to be a medical missionary!"

Shocked by the news Mrs. Mowrer rose quickly and headed toward her bedroom to keep Angelika from seeing her cry. Rather than follow, Angelika gave her time to regain her composure.

Shortly after, her mother returned to the table and said, "I have seen a change in you for the last few months, but I didn't know you had such plans."

"I know you want me to study music, and my school advisor said that if I go to the University of Vienna I can study medicine with a minor in music. I know without a doubt that God has called me to be a doctor."

"I'm sure you are listening to the Lord, Dear, but why a missionary? You could be a doctor right here in Salzburg," reasoned Mrs. Mowrer.

"It's not just being a doctor. The Lord has called me to help the poor also. I believe they deserve an education and healing in their lives. So many people need a physical healing and a spiritual healing."

"And when you say 'missionary' I wonder where you plan on going." "I have been doing a lot of studying and praying." Watching her mother closely she slowly added, "I believe the Lord is leading me to Southeast Asia."

"Asia? I don't know if I can accept it. I'm sure the Lord is right, but we've been inseparable for so long, and I am very selfish of my time with you. Please be patient with me as I try to adjust."

Mrs. Mowrer hugged her daughter and assured her that they would make it through whatever the Lord placed in their paths.

Angelika spent the remaining months before graduation working out the final details of college with her parents. Her mother was reluctant to admit the decision was the right one, but her father knew she was very smart and capable.

Graduation day was one of rejoicing by family and friends as

Angelika graduated second in her class. Shortly after the ceremony her school advisor sought her out of the crowd.

"You have the capacity to succeed in the same ways Albert Schweitzer did if you work hard and train for it. Schweitzer built a hospital and facilities on his compound at Lambarene in French Equatorial Africa that had more than 80 buildings. He was a doctor and surgeon in the hospital, pastor of the congregation, Administrator of the village and a writer of scholarly books. You can do the same thing," he concluded.

"Thank you for all your help and support." Angelika graciously shook her advisor's hand.

As she turned to walk away, he stopped her. "I do believe you need this," he said smiling as he handed her the envelope containing her acceptance letter for studies at the University of Vienna. Jumping with joy, Angelika ran to her parents with the news of her acceptance.

Now the blessing of hard work and a concentration on her studies had paid off, along with her firm belief God was setting a goal she had to focus on.

The summer months went quickly as she and her parents shopped for clothes and packed all the necessary items Angelika would need for her move.

Her Journey Begins

The day for Angelika's departure to the University finally arrived. Her entire family and a number of friends gathered at the train station. Hugs were in abundance and tears plentiful, but they saw this as a milestone for each to remember.

The minister gathered the family together and said a prayer. Angelika remembered part of it as the train whistle blew its departure: "Your hand is on this precious young lady. Direct her path."

The ride was pleasant and exciting for Angelika as she headed toward a future yet unknown to her. The backdrop was stunning and typically Austrian. Pastel villages were tucked in the rolling green hills and punctuated by the requisite churches. The countryside was full of breathtaking views, very green and picturesque, making the scenery on the ride amazing to her.

She was taking in the entire Austrian countryside sprinkled with quaint houses with flower boxes full of blooming red flowers hanging from the outside window sills. Many homes also had cattle, all fully equipped with ringing and clanking bells for the farmer to always be able to hear where his animals were. Even from the train she seemed to hear them ring.

The three and a half hour trip passed quickly for her, but her mind was still thinking of home and the journey into a new venture in Vienna. She was determined to enjoy every day and apply herself to her studies in such a way to make the Lord proud of her. She had come so far already and did not want to disappoint Him.

Her first four years at the University of Vienna turned out to be exciting and full of many long hours studying. She took all her premedical classes seriously, but still enjoyed playing long hours on the piano and organ for her music minor and for her own simple enjoyment.

Angelika was also very popular and her maturing beauty made many of the male classmates rally toward her. While her goal was to finish school and do well, she did date occasionally.

She dated Johann Draby, a fellow classmate, and he went to church with her a number of times, but didn't profess any belief in a supreme being. When she began to have some interest in him, she was reminded of her goal to become a medical missionary. After discussing this with Johann, because she detected he did not want any of this in his future, so they decided to just remain friends.

Angelika was very loyal to her new church and was often invited to meals at the minister's home. His wife had become a second mother to her and was often known to advise her about serious situations.

The head pastor of the church asked if he could introduce her to another student that attended from time to time. "I think you have a lot in common. You both like music," he had told her.

Anton Musbaugh was a very nice guy, but he wanted romance much faster than Angelika desired. He was a very handsome music major, and even though she admitted to herself that she had some interest in him a number of times, realizing once again it would lead her away from her goal, she had to stop his advances.

He once said to her, "I can't get to first base with you."

She had responded with, "I just want to go slow at this time. We have just met and hardly know each other."

Anton was a very good pianist, but as many artists of his level, also very temperamental. At a recital one evening, Angelika was proud of how well he was playing. When he missed a couple notes he suddenly blew up and left the stage. At the tea shop afterwards, the incident was all Anton could talk about. Angelika decided that his temper was more than she wanted to handle in a marriage.

Thanking God that she had been spared another detour to her goal in life, Angelika decided to stop dating. She would often enjoy a concert or opera, but went only with a friend whose company she enjoyed and had no motive beyond that evening.

Angelika's dedication and focus earned her high scores in all her classes. She graduated third in her class with two separate awards. One was for a medical research project and another for her musical ability.

Her parents were very pleased with her accomplishments, but Mrs. Mowrer was still holding on to the hope that Angelika would not continue pursuing a degree in medicine.

"You know it just doesn't seem like four years have passed, although your father and I have missed you so. I do hope you are ready to come back home and teach music. You know, our church organist is getting old and you could have her job."

"Mother, the decision for my future has already been made. I wouldn't be happy going back home to teach music. God needs me to go to His chosen place, and with my acceptance into the medical division here at the university, I find myself looking even more forward to the day I can go to Asia."

"I know, my dear. Your letters are always so full of joy. I guess I just worry about how lonely you will be."

"I'll not be alone with my Lord, Mother. You know that. You are the one who taught me He would be with me in all situations. Besides, I still have four years right here. God may send me a husband during that time, but let's not think about that right now. Let's go celebrate."

Angelika had no idea who God might select as her helpmate, but she trusted that He had someone with whom she could do her life's calling.

Knowing that she needed to get her education and training behind her, she was in no hurry to mess up God's plan for her.

A Helpmate Is Needed

Malin Rasmussen had recently graduated from a university in his hometown of Graz. His parents were both nurses, and he wanted to follow them into the medical field. He had chosen to enter school at the Medical University of Vienna due to its famous history in the medical field. He knew without having an important family name in medicine, he would have to have a highly recognized degree to obtain a position in an accredited hospital or practice.

Malin's parents were not very well fixed financially, and he had to work hard and seek assistance to earn his medical degree. Because of his interest in medicine, he found help easily from the government of his country in the form of grants and scholarships.

He was also fortunate to be going to school in the same city as his close friend Karl Brendel. The two decided to live off campus and share an apartment. They found a three story complex which gave them room for themselves and allowed the rental of the additional rooms to other students. This produced more than enough money to pay the rent and have some extras for essentials.

While the two had different interests it caused no problems in sharing the ownership of the apartment building. Each designed his own room for study in his field. Karl, a music major and avid pianist, soundproofed his room so he could play his piano and other instruments. Malin lined his room with many book shelves to store his medical books and the text books his parents had shared with him. He also made sure to get a comfortable chair and desk as he knew he would be spending all of his available time studying.

During his second year at the university, as fate would have it, he met Angelika. They both had selected the same medical professor and shared the same demands of a first year resident doctor.

Over the next few months they found themselves spending a

lot of time together moving from one university clinic to another. The hours were tiring and they never had many opportunities to sit down and get to know each other. Angelika, however, could sense Malin's desire to socialize.

Approaching him at lunch one day she asked, "Would you like to sit with me in the cafeteria today?"

Malin was a shy person, but forgot that as he blurted out, "I sure would!"

Malin thought Angelika was the most beautiful girl he had ever met.

Because he was afraid he could not compete for her, he had been guarding himself from doing something foolish. He was very glad for this opportunity to spend personal time with Angelika.

When they were comfortably seated, Malin asked Angelika why she had chosen the medical profession.

"I have felt the Lord calling me to be a medical missionary. I have done a lot of research and know that I want to go somewhere in Southeast Asia to help the poor people with their medical and spiritual needs," Angelika confidently answered.

Malin was so shocked by her answer that he could only utter an awed "Wow!" He knew that Angelika was a special person. He had sensed an incredible level of compassion when he watched her with patients, but the information she just shared with him was quite profound. His goals seemed so dim compared with what she had just told him, and his fear of not being good enough for her deepened.

Angelika, unaware of Malin's line of thought, easily continued the conversation. "What do you feel the Lord has called you to do with your medical career?"

"Well," Malin began hesitantly, "I'm not sure the Lord has called me to anything. I just always assumed I would return home and work in the local hospital or maybe in a private practice. Nothing as special as what you will be doing."

"Oh, Malin," interrupted Angelika, "Any time you can help others in this world you are doing something special."

Malin truly fell in love with Angelika over lunch that day. Her beauty ran deep, and Malin was so impressed with her humble sincerity.

Unbeknownst to him at the time, Angelika felt drawn more to Malin than any other man she had ever dated.

Angelika, who had not actively pursued a dating lifestyle, found herself rather surprised when she realized she was falling in love with a fellow classmate.

The two continued to gravitate to each other as they prepared for their lessons or discussed the diagnoses of patients. They began spending more of their free time together and enjoyed sharing stories of the past and discussed their present and future aspirations. They had like spirits and both appreciated each others' intelligence.

One evening after several long hours of studying, Malin reached over and took Angelika's hand. Looking her right in the eye, he said, "I believe I've fallen in love with you."

Even though she found herself wanting a stronger relationship with Malin, Angelika was concerned about getting too serious. She was afraid it would detour her commitment to the medical mission field.

"Malin, I would be lying if I didn't admit to feeling the same way, but you know I plan on going to Asia, and I can't let anything, or anyone, get in the way of the Lord's plan for me." Angelika was close to tears, but she would remain firm to her faith in the Lord.

"I know," Malin meekly replied. "I don't want to lose you. You know I'm not certain about God and a 'calling' from Him, but I've been doing a lot of thinking, and I'm quite certain about one thing. If our relationship continues to grow, I want to go to Asia with you."

"Malin," began Angelika hesitantly, "Do you realize what a commitment you would be making? I've had years to study, plan and adjust to the idea of what life in Southeast Asia will be like. You've had only a brief period of time. I admire what you are saying, but you can't make a hasty decision."

"I've done nothing but think about going, and I want to be the one that goes to help you." Malin spoke with more force than usual, and Angelika realized how very serious he was. She chose her next words very carefully.

"Since we are talking about a possible future, there is one more thing that I must share and discuss with you. You know how strong my faith in the Lord is. I have a personal relationship with Him, and I know I will not be able to accomplish anything in Asia if I don't follow His guidance. I don't believe we can take our relationship much further without you committing to Him also."

Malin was overwhelmed by her requirement, but didn't want to see a separation between them. With her soft hand in his, he contemplated what she was asking of him then shyly spoke, "I don't know much about this religious stuff since I was not raised in a church, but I do believe there is a God. If you will be patient with me, I will ask if you will teach me about your religion. I don't want to lose you. I want to do this with you."

Angelika took his other hand also and looking lovingly into his eyes she simply said, "Together."

God's Match Is Made

Angelika and Malin had spent all their time together with their studies, but as they fell more deeply in love, they arranged to be together in their free time also. Angelika had been attending a nearby church for the past seven years and Malin began regularly joining her. It was a good teaching church and the ministers excelled in explaining the Bible and the Gospel to the attendees.

Angelika had arranged for Malin to take some of the doctrinal classes taught by one of the ministers at the church. The first course he took was entitled "The Apostles Creed," which really enlightened him since its foundation came directly from the close followers of Jesus Christ. Since Malin had no religious background he wanted proof for nearly every doctrine, and this course really helped him.

He was extremely aware that the theological specifics of the creed appeared to have been originally formulated as a refutation of Gnosticism, an early heresy. He saw the creed stated that Christ Jesus, was born, suffered, and died on the cross. This seemed to be a statement directly against the heretical teaching that Christ only appeared to become man and that he did not truly suffer and die, but only appeared to do so.

The minister teaching the course said the name of the creed probably came from the fifth-century legend that, under the inspiration of the Holy Spirit after Pentecost, each of the twelve apostles dictated part of it and was traditionally divided into twelve articles. Malin believed The Apostles Creed was esteemed as an example of the apostles' teachings and a defense of the Gospel of Christ.

Malin wrote and carried around the creed:

I believe in God, the Father Almighty, maker of Heaven and Earth.

And in Jesus Christ, His only Son, our Lord, who was conceived by the Holy Spirit, born of the Virgin Mary, suffered under Pontius Pilate, was crucified, died and was buried.

He descended into Hell. The third day He rose again from the dead.

He ascended into Heaven and sits at the right hand of God the Father Almighty.

From thence He will come to judge the living and the dead. I believe in the Holy Spirit, the holy Christian Church, the communion of saints, the forgiveness of sins, the resurrection of the body, and the life everlasting. Amen.

Malin began to memorize each verse in order to build his own belief in Christ, but He was finding it hard to grasp each concept about Christianity and couldn't see the need to turn his life completely over to the Lord. He knew Angelika was disappointed, even though she would have never voiced that to him, and so he decided to approach her one Sunday afternoon.

"Angelika, I know that you were hoping I would get as involved in religion as you are, but I just don't believe that I have to turn my life completely over to Him. I am really sorry if I have disappointed you."

"Malin, I can see the changes you have made in your beliefs about an almighty creator, and I am very glad about that. The Creator that you believe in now is the same creator that made you. He created you for a special roll in this life, and I know that you can fulfill it with greatness. The only disappointment I have is that you consider God just 'religion.' Knowing our Creator is not just a list of theological concepts, but it is a relationship between two. It is my hope that you would one day feel as close to Him as you do to me."

Malin, in contemplative thought, quietly answered, "I'm not sure if that will ever happen. Can you still love me?"

"Always, and I will continue to pray that you might find the key to unlock a greater relationship than the one we share."

Malin, saddened by his disappointing Angelika, tried his hardest in other areas to strengthen their relationship. He often took her to the opera and other musical concerts in their free time, and while he didn't necessarily like the classical music, he wanted to spend every available moment with the woman he loved.

Malin's parents didn't often get to visit, but the next time they came he made a special point for them to meet Angelika. The meeting was a pleasant one, and they became friends immediately.

Angelika was amazed at how close he was to his parents and how much he was built and looked like his father. She learned that both had been soccer players and were quite athletic, and like Malin, his father had continued to keep in excellent condition.

Malin's mother was a very sweet woman and showed her kindness to Angelika from the very beginning.

Malin could tell they really liked his girlfriend, and he was pleased they were showing her special attention even though he had never confided his strong feelings to them.

His parents were moved by her beauty, but even more by her intelligence and compassion. They had never been around anyone whose religion was as much a part of one's life as was hers.

After learning of Angelika's plans for her future, they were concerned their son would be giving up financial security if he chose to marry her and go to Asia. They could tell that Angelika would not be moved from the future she called "God's calling." They trusted their son however, and would willingly give their blessing if she was the girl he chose.

Angelika's parents were scheduled to visit at the end of the week, and when Malin found out that the visit would overlap with his parents', he asked her if they could plan a get-together for them to meet. Angelika readily agreed and immediately called one of their favorite restaurants to reserve enough room for the two families.

Malin grew concerned as to whether his family would fit in with Angelika's, and the day they were to meet he shared his thoughts.

"I'm not sure how well my mom and dad will fit in with your family. Your dad is so successful with his business and your mother is such a genteel woman."

"Malin, my parents are just people like yours. I know they will fall in love with your family as quickly as I have. I don't think you have a thing to be concerned with," was her sympathetic reply.

Her prophesy was correct as they all gathered in the restaurant. The two families mixed and communicated the whole evening. Malin and Angelika were delighted as everyone hugged goodbye and made plans to sit together at the graduation that was just two months away. It was apparent that they had seen the beginning of a good relationship between both family units.

As Angelika's mother hugged her she whispered in her ear, "You are going to marry him aren't you?"

Angelika's reply was a big smile. "I hope so," she softly admitted.

It was less than a week later that Angelika called home to tell her mother that Malin had proposed. Mrs. Mowrer, having previously known, since Malin had asked Mr. Mowrer for permission on their recent visit, acted greatly surprised and was genuinely happy.

The day came when Angelika and Malin's long sought goal was achieved. Both had been outstanding students and had made a number of accomplishments in the medical school. Each was considered an outstanding student by their team of medical professors, and both graduated with honors.

As they gathered with their friends after the ceremony, they each shared their final well-wishes. "Malin and the soon-to-be Mrs.

Dr. Rasmussen," began a fellow graduate. "Man, I still can't believe you would give up so much here in Austria to care for those poor people who can't even pay you for your help."

Malin took Angelika's hand. They had faced that same thought from other friends who had gone into the medical profession to make a good living. Malin just smiled as Angelika gave her familiar and heart-warming reply. "I am doing what God called me to do."

"Yes, but what did God call YOU to do, Malin?" asked another.

Inside he was still confused about where God was supposed to fit into his life, so jokingly Malin answered, "Wouldn't you follow a beauty like Angelika wherever she went?"

The Two Become One

Angelika had been delighted when she received approval to be married in the Salzburg Cathedral. Mozart's parents had been married there, he had been baptized there, and he had served there as court organist. The local bishop had to give his permission to be wed in the Cathedral because the Mowrer family was known as loyal Protestants. The approval fulfilled a lifelong dream of Angelika's, and as she stood in her beautiful white dress covered with lace and a long train fanned out behind her, she thanked her Lord for all the blessings He had given her.

As her two sisters, serving as duo bridesmaids, began their slow walk up the aisle Angelika's father took her hands. With tears streaming down his face, Mr. Mowrer kissed Angelika's cheek and whispered, "I'm so proud of you."

Malin, Karl, who served as the best man, and Angelika's pastor entered from the side room from behind the pulpit. Malin was so contented that this day had finally come. Years of dating and discussing the future were now to become a reality. He couldn't help but smile as he watched Angelika and her father approaching. He met them, hands outstretched, and received Angelika from her father. With a handshake and a heartfelt, "Thank you," Malin escorted his lovely bride up the four steps to meet the minister.

"If you are ready to enter the estate of marriage," began the minister, "you may do so by joining right hands."

The beautiful old church was filled with friends and family as they observed the ceremony to unite the couple in marriage.

"Malin, do you take this woman to be your lawful and true wedded wife, to love her in sickness or in health, in joy or in pain and to cleave unto her only as long as you both shall live?"

Malin quickly replied, "Yes, I will."

The question was asked of Angelika who replied in the same manner as Malin.

The minister continued by asking Malin what he had as a token of his pledge.

"A ring."

He was directed by the minister to take the ring and place it on the third finger of her left hand. The minister noted that the ring finger was believed by early Greeks to contain a nerve that ran to the heart. Then he asked Malin to repeat after him: "With this ring, given to thee, as a token of my love, I seal my vows, I thee wed, in the name of the Father, the Son, and the Holy Spirit."

When Malin finished repeating the vow, the minister instructed, "You may kiss the bride." As the two shared an emotional kiss, the minister loudly concluded, "May I introduce to you Mr. and Mrs. Malin Rasmussen."

Applause and cheers echoed through the auditorium even as the new husband and wife began their exit to the foyer of the church. Afterwards friends gathered to greet the wedding families and to share in the cake and punch. Congratulations were given and most of the conversation was concerning their soon departure for Asia.

It wasn't long before the couple changed from their wedding attire, kissed their parents goodbye and boarded a car for a honeymoon in Germany.

While traveling through Germany they drove into some of the most attractive and interesting towns. After a night in Munich they departed after brunch and arrived in Oberammergau where the buildings and homes were all painted with beautiful frescoes depicting the history and religion of the quaint mountain village nestled in the Bavarian Alps.

As they strode about town, they noticed that the shops were unique with items not viewed in many other shops they had previously explored. Down one of the streets they saw what appeared to be a large building that seemed totally out of place with the rest of the town. They inquired of a shop keeper who told them that was the place where the city citizens presented a passion play every ten years and the next presentation was scheduled to begin the next day.

In their room later that evening they found a pamphlet full of information regarding the passion play. This little village was in danger of losing all its inhabitants due to the Black Plague during the Thirty Years War, so the elders of the town met, prayed, and vowed that if the village would be spared they would present a pageant depicting the last days of the life of Jesus Christ. The town was spared and thus the beginning of such an event. The first play was in 1634, and the town had done a performance every ten years since.

Angelika was very excited about seeing such a live performance and found it difficult to sleep. Malin, too, was excited. He was striving to continue to learn as much as possible about Jesus, and he was intrigued by the faith an entire town could have in such a man.

Waking at first daylight, the couple prepared for the day and arrived in the already crowded street to watch the pageant that would begin at 9 a.m. and continue till 5:30 that evening.

At first they were both a little skeptical about the length of the play, but as soon as the play began they were overwhelmed by the huge cast of actors and animals. Their program stated there would be 2,155 participants to move across the beautiful set. The play was so expertly crafted that the closing scene came too early for the newlyweds.

That night they shared many of the thoughts and emotions that they experienced throughout the day. Angelika was glad to share more of her faith with her husband who she could tell had been greatly influenced that day.

As they opened the Bible in their room for their nightly devotion, it opened to a verse that became the challenge of their future lives:

"For the preaching of the cross is to them that perish foolishness; but unto us who believe it is the power of God." --1 Corinthians 1:18.

Her Dream Begins

Angelika had finished her research and with much debate, she and Malin decided they would go to Laos. Now their tickets, passports, and visas were all complete, and the date of departure had finally arrived. They had packed very little, knowing they would need to send for the rest of their needed belongings when they had an established location.

The scene at the airport was very teary. Angelika clung to her mother and father not sure of when or if she would ever see them again.

"Thank you for always supporting and encouraging me. You have always believed in me, and your love has helped make me what I am today. Please make sure you pray for us each day. We will try and write as often as we can. Don't forget us."

Angelika's mother smiled through her tears, "You know good and well that you will not be forgotten. My dear, Angelika, you have always made your father and me proud. The people of Laos will be very blessed to have you. We know that you will accomplish much for our Lord. God go with you, my daughter."

Mr. Mowrer grabbed his oldest daughter in a tight hug. He was afraid to speak through the tears that were threatening to overwhelm him. "I love you, Daddy," Angelika managed. Her father's response was to tighten his embrace.

Malin's family was a mirror of emotions. As they held each other as one Mrs. Rasmussen smiled lovingly at her only son. "We are a little jealous of the people in Laos for getting you when your life is just beginning. You are a wonderful man, and we just wish there was more time. We will see you and your bride again. Best of luck."

"I love you both very much." Through many tears Malin continued, "You have given me such opportunities in life. Without your support I wouldn't have been able to achieve such success in medical school. I hope that I am not disappointing you."

Mr. Rasmussen confided, "Your mother and I always figured we would have the privilege of working side-by-side with you one day. Disappointed? We couldn't be more proud of you, Son. You are a fabulous doctor, and we believe that you will do great things for improving the medicine in Laos. Good luck."

Malin turned to Angelika. He knew that while she was overjoyed with her dreams coming true, her heart was also breaking with having to leave her family. Taking her gently by the arm and slowly guiding her away he whispered in her ear, "Let's go home."

Angelika, overwhelmed with his understanding, managed to answer, "Yes," as she took his hand and prepared to board the first plane taking them from Vienna, Austria to Vientiane, Laos.

Knowing there would be many stops; Angelika researched each city and found places to tour if there was time allotted. The first stop was in the capital city of Budapest, Hungary, known for its architectural style, amazingly diverse restaurants, Gypsy music and friendly people.

Their layover was for four hours so Malin and Angelika were able to tour some of the city. They knew much of the history of this country since it was once one of the largest kingdoms in Europe. However, signs of deterioration were evident after it had suffered through many centuries of invasions, unwanted occupation, and a world war.

Even though they were excited to get to Laos, their time for sightseeing was over too quickly. They boarded a larger plane, and since their flight to T'Bilisi, Georgia would be longer than their first, they tried to sleep as much as possible.

Not realizing their flight would take them over the rugged Caucasus Mountains, the two were amazed at the beautiful sight below them. While flying above and through the mountains were quite a shaking experience, the pilot made it very interesting by sharing several facts.

"To the left you can get a glimpse of Mt. Kasbek, Georgia's highest point at 16,558 feet. Europe's highest point, Mt.Elbrus, is located just over Georgia's northern border to the right of Kasbek. It reaches 18,841 feet," he offered.

··························ıı‖ııı····················

After landing in T'Bilisi they knew their next flight would not leave till the morning so Malin and Angelika, although travel weary, decided to take in another tour. In front of the airport Malin flagged a taxi and handed the driver a hand written note that read, "The Paliashvill Opera House." Angelika had underlined that particular sight in her tour book as a "must see."

In about thirty minutes they pulled in front of a quite impressive building. A guide inside told them it was built in 1851 and had become the most important symbol of the city's cultural life. After a quick tour of the beautiful building they rushed back to the airport to meet the airline personnel in order to be checked into a hotel for the night.

They welcomed a good meal and comfortable bed, and after their refreshing night's sleep, the Rasmussens awoke ready to finish their long journey.

Their first flight for the day would take them to Delhi, India. After an hour in the air they began to cross the Caspian Sea located on the eastern edge of Europe. Malin remarked to Angelika, "This is the largest lake on the planet, and by looking at this map, it will take quite a while to get to the other coast in Turkmenistan."

The flight, including one stop for fuel, was their longest yet. Upon arriving in Delhi they made their final change of planes. They would make one more stop in Mandalay, Burma before reaching Vientiane, Laos and catching a commuter plane from there.

There had been numerous stops in lands unfamiliar to the Rasmussens, but they took the long trip without fear, knowing that

God was their protector in this new stage of their lives. Being this close to their final destination was hard. They were anxious to finish their short commuter flight to Savannakhet.

Vientiane, Laos would have been a disappointment if they had compared it to the other places they had stopped, but they knew touring was not the reason for coming. They were set on making this land their home to help the poor and helpless.

Laos was a low-key French protectorate, known as the land of the lotus-eaters, where an indolent lifestyle prevailed. It was too mountainous for plantations, there was little in the way of mining, and the MekongRiver was not suitable for commercial navigation.

The French built very few roads. The main colonial route constructed was from the city of Luang Prabang through Vientiane to Savannakhet and the Cambodian frontier. Angelika had done her research and selected Savannakhet, the second-largest city in Laos, to live in while they made plans for the location of a medical clinic.

Upon reaching the Savannakhet airport they found taxi drivers in abundance. They carefully selected a decent looking vehicle since many of the cars didn't look like they could get out the gate.

They entered a hotel shortly after nightfall and spent extra time in prayer before retiring that night. "Dear Lord," Angelika led, "You have kept us safe through our travels and we thank you for that. Please help guide our next steps in helping your people of this land. We pray that you will give us wisdom about this land and the people we need to speak with. We further pray that you will open all the doors that need to be opened for our success in this mission."

The next morning the Rasmussen doctors set out through town to learn as much about the area as possible. Over the next three days they learned a great deal by talking with the locals and business owners.

They discovered that there were several main sections to the city. The old French colonial quarter of the town, along the Mekong riverfront, was depressed and crumbling. The town's proximity to Thailand's booming economy had brought about new commercial development in the northern area of the town near the river crossing.

Like all Lao cities, Savannakhet had a mixed population of Lao, Thai, Vietnamese and Chinese, as well as minority peoples from the Lao interior. It had a large 15 There was no protestant community as the religion was mostly unknown.

Malin and Angelika made arrangements to meet several government officials and other leaders in the area. They explained their reasoning for being in the area and asked for assistance in locating the best place to build their clinic. The officials and leaders were very helpful and excited that someone would be able to help the distressed area.

While Malin and Angelika were not in any hurry, since this was to be a life commitment, the officials seemed to know the exact location where they needed to set up their clinic.

"About 35 miles north of here is a place where there is no medical care. There is no place to train the many in need of vocational or academic help," advised one government official. "Come. We will go today," he concluded.

It didn't take Malin long to get caught up in the excitement, and he was surprised to see Angelika acting so reserved. He gave her a questioning look, and as soon as she had an opportunity to speak privately to him she said, "I don't want to rush before the Lord. I have to know that this is where He wants us. I'm afraid there are too many decisions being made today."

After going as far as they could in the car, the small party continued on foot. As they went they learned that the area represented one of the world's great cultural boundaries with the division line between the Indianized world of most of mainland Southeast Asia: Burma, Thailand, Laos, and Cambodia and the Sinicized world of China, Korea, Japan, and Vietnam. For thousands of years, people on the different sides of this cultural divide followed different cultural styles and world views. The doctors were thinking what a challenge would be before them if this was the area the Lord had chosen.

Arriving at mid-day they were able to meet many of the community leaders. Their self-appointed guide enthusiastically told of the doctors' mission for their area, and the leaders became excited about the prospects of a medical center. They immediately began talking amongst themselves about how they could help get the land and resources to build such a place.

The leaders questioned Malin and Angelika almost faster than they could answer. It wasn't long before Angelika gave Malin a wink. He knew that she had her answer of where the clinic would be located, and he was comforted to see the look of peace that she so easily wore.

Before they left to go back to the city, the community leaders promised to begin making arrangements for the doctors' clinic and said they would send word whenever all the details had been arranged.

By the end of the week the Rasmussens were invited back to the remote area for the elders and leaders to give them a detailed report. The doctors discovered that not only was a clinic to be built, but an entire compound was proposed. The land had already been chosen and donated, and the locals had agreed to assist in the building. The building materials were also being provided by the locals who were willing to do whatever they could to help.

The next day the Rasmussens moved into a small room at one of the leader's homes in the remote village. The plans would be finished that day, and the building would begin the very next.

Months passed, the compound buildings were taking shape, and the doctors were ready to do what they had come to do. They knew their house was scheduled to be completed first, so they had written home to have their small boxes of belongings sent along with a supply of medicines and medical equipment that had been chosen before they left.

The day to dedicate the facility had finally come and many excited people from area villages attended. The clinic was in the center of the compound with the teaching auditorium behind it. The Rasmussens' home and a dorm-like building for the help were on the opposite side of the grounds. Another building for the displaced was in the plans as need for it became necessary.

The doctors were introduced by the leader of the community. Then another of the elders, with the immediate attention of the others spoke, "This is a memorable day for us. A wonderful thing has been established for our people, and we have joined together in friendship to see this work completed. I would like to suggest we call it 'Friendship Mission.'"

Dr. Malin explained their ministry, "The original purpose of Friendship Mission is to attend to the needs of those living near the Mission and for those who cannot pay for medical help. We plan to begin teaching programs as soon as possible." And with that, Friendship Mission was founded in 1930 by the combined efforts of the community and the two doctors.

As the months passed, Friendship Mission grew in vitality and the outreach of its programs expanded. Besides offering basic services to poor families, the Mission clinic was an important ministry and the school provided educational opportunities for the community children and adults.

Doctors Malin and Angelika had become well respected in the area and for years had become mainstays in the community. They had saved many of the families from sure death, and they had shared the love of Jesus with all they met.

Their reputation had spread even into many of the cities in the region with government and country leadership praising the efforts of the clinic and training compound.

Now thirty years later the people of the area continued to show respect and protection for the clinic. They had built a number of homes for the displaced and needy as promised. Hundreds of children and displaced families had been cared for, trained, and sent on to do a productive work elsewhere. The ones that stayed were great helpers in the mission and clinic.

By now the compound had grown to be much like a city of its own and the community felt, due to the continuing threat of warmongers, they should encircle the compound with a wall for its protection. With the use of the abundance of elephants and timber in the area, the project did not take but a few months.

The Start Of Friendship Mission

Malin and Angelika had worked all those years in Friendship Mission offering medicine and training to both body and mind. They had never complained during the days of struggle. From the very offset of the mission, they knew a mighty strength was leading them, and therefore chose to stay in the continuous war-torn country. They had only returned home once during their thirty years' ministry due to the demands on their time. Their families had visited numerous times from Austria, but they were getting old themselves and hoped their children would return to live near them again.

The call of God was too heavy a burden for the doctors, and they refused to leave their faraway home. They had known joy and periods of sadness. The stress and long hours required at the mission were beginning to affect them both.

"Are you sorry you came with me to this place, Malin?" Angelika asked during their evening time of solitude.

"I would have never been happy anywhere else, but with you," he assured her.

"We are now in our fifties, and I have a growing concern as to who will follow us," she wistfully stated.

Her remark to Marlin seemed to be a plea. Somehow she may have had a fear her job would not be finished.

During their time at Friendship Mission, Angelika had given birth to three children. Sadly, two lived only a short time and one was stillborn. They were buried in a private plot nearby where Malin and Angelika could walk each evening to sit, talk, and enjoy the majestic vistas.

The two had hoped for another child who would live and bring happiness to them, but their hopes had faded as age took over. It was a short time after their conversation about the future that Angelika discovered she was pregnant. She and Malin were very excited, but cautious. With her past history and her present age, the doctors knew that many problems could arise.

It was on one of their evening walks to the cemetery that Angelika dared to dream, "Malin, just think of all the wonderful things we can share with our child. All our friends here will spoil her rotten."

"Her?" Malin asked with a raise of his eyebrows. "What makes you so sure that our friends won't be teaching our son how to get into mischief?"

Laughing, the two continued walking hand in hand. They had never felt more in love than they did at this time in their lives.

"I think we should name him Paul," suggested Malin. "Since Paul was such a great missionary just like our son's mother. Or perhaps we should name him Luke, since his mother is such a great doctor."

Malin glanced at Angelika and saw that a funny look had come over her face.

"Well, there are plenty other names to choose from if you don't like those." "Malin," Angelika interrupted. "Something is wrong. I'm suddenly having strong abdominal cramps. Get me back to the clinic."

As Angelika grabbed her stomach and doubled over in pain, Malin gently swept her up into his arms and headed for the clinic. With each step Malin could hear her praying, "Oh God, please don't take my baby. Please, God, don't take our baby again."

Coming into sight of the compound, Malin yelled for Ling. Ling, a nurse assistant had escaped from China and had been a trusted worker assisting Dr. Angelika from the very first day he and his brothers had come to the compound. She had treated him so kindly, and they shared a special bond.

When he saw Dr. Malin carrying Dr. Angelika, he ran to the hospital to prepare a bed for her.

Ling did all he could to make Dr. Angelika comfortable as Malin checked all her vital signs. She appeared to be very healthy, and yet neither doctor could determine what had caused the cramps and why they were not going away. Within an hour Angelika went into labor with their fourth child. Her strength was disappearing fast, and she knew that Malin was scared.

"Malin, dear," she whispered. "I love you. I have loved you from the very beginning. I can't thank you enough for taking this journey with me. Next to God, you have been my everything. I believe it is time for me to meet Him face to face."

Malin tried to stop her. He wanted to argue and tell her she was wrong.

"Shh, my love," Angelika continued. "You know that I will be in a better place, and I will be waiting for you. Don't blame the Lord for the way He has chosen to end our journey. Continue on the journey with Him. Trust Him completely and continue building your relationship with Him. He never once led us astray in this wilderness. He won't do it in the future either. Remember our love."

Malin, giving in to the truth, wrapped Angelika in his arms and held her through the pain. Ling continued silently doing whatever he could to make her comfortable.

"Ling," she managed to say. "I have had a better life from knowing you. Thank you for all you have done for me. I love you, too."

Ling began to answer Dr. Angelika, but she had closed her eyes and slipped into eternity.

After placing Angelika comfortably once more on the bed Dr. Malin and Ling shared several minutes of grief.

"Ling," Dr. Malin quietly spoke. "Would you and your brothers dig the grave? Please, leave one last place for me."

Ling quietly left to get Lang and Noi. When they returned to the compound they went to get Dr. Malin who was still sitting vigilantly by

Dr. Angelika's side.

"Dr. Malin, the grave is ready and a box has been donated for Dr. Angelika's body. The whole village has begun to gather. We will be ready for the burial when you are."

Before Ling could leave the room, Dr. Malin asked him to please help him carry her body out to the box. "We will bury our daughter with her."

Unbeknownst to Malin, one of Angelika's loyal friends had brought a beautifully woven blanket and laid it on the foot of the bed. Ling helped him wrap his beloved wife and infant daughter in the blanket and then carried them out to the box. Another friend had lined the box with a bed of soft vines. While the lid was being nailed in place, Malin returned to the office to get Angelika's Bible.

As some of the village men carried Dr. Angelika's burial box, Malin followed behind reading some of her favorite scriptures.

At the gravesite, Dr. Malin was so proud of Angelika. The show of support from the number of villagers was proof that she was an outstanding woman. Many were openly weeping as they watched the men place her into the grave.

"Would anyone like to say anything?" the doctor asked.

Ling spoke first, "Dr. Angelika Rasmussen was like a second mother to me. She had a heart of trust that could only come from God. She reminded me of my real mother who was also filled with the Lord. I am grateful to have known her." Ling bowed his head and sobbed uncontrollably.

Everyone bowed in prayer asking God to provide strength for Dr. Malin.

After the burial plot was filled, all walked back to the clinic except for Malin, who remained. He sat with his face in his hands, as he had done many times before, looking at the graves of all his beloved family. He already realized how lonely he now was and would be.

Malin lamented over the loss of Angelika.

"O, Angelika!

"O, Angelika!

"I don't know what I will do without you.

"You were all I ever lived for.

"O, Angelika.

"My beloved one, my love, my joy.

"I will always love you."

Wiping the tears from his eyes he rose and began to walk slowly back toward the clinic, stopping occasionally to weep.

The next day Dr. Rasmussen appeared at the hospital to make his rounds. He knew returning to the lifework he had shared with his wife would be good therapy. The staff ran up to him, as if to console him, but he stopped each by giving them instructions as to what needed to be done.

Malin's name meant, "Little Warrior," and it reflected a trait that fit him correctly, since he never gave up the struggle for the people of the mission. In spite of the conflicts all around, he was unafraid.

A Wilderness Life

Ling remembered the early days living at the mission with the Rasmussens. The doctors had quickly found the boys jobs to do. They discovered that this was a working facility, and each person had to help with the chores.

Dr. Angelika liked the mannerisms of the brothers. After her query into the past of the two oldest, she learned Ling had some minor training in medicine and both had worked in a small hospital. What a joy this was to the Rasmussens. Experience and consistency from workers in the clinic were lacking.

Ling and his brothers had been taught a strong work ethic. After a few months the doctors knew the boys could be trusted and had found favor with the doctors.

The boys loved living and working in their new homeland, and while they often remembered and missed their Chinese parents, they had learned to fend for themselves and put more of their trust in the Lord.

Their Christian upbringing helped them have a closer relationship with the Rasmussens, too, especially Angelika. Ling felt lost with Dr. Angelika gone, and he was grateful for the company and help he received from a new volunteer named Ping, a quiet, but capable young lady who accompanied him on his rounds each day.

Ping was a beautiful young lady and very trim in her nurse's uniform.

She didn't seem to fit in with the others around the compound. It was obvious she hadn't worked doing hard chores in her youth. She didn't have rough hands or a worn face. She did, however, have a great desire to learn more about caring for others.

There Will Be Someone to Follow Us

One morning, while entering Allen's room, Ling introduced Ping. "She will be joining me in my rounds each morning."

Allen noted immediately how gracious and kind Ping was, and he was glad to discover that she also spoke English. Ling shared how the two of them were glad to have someone with which they could keep their English fresh.

Allen learned in a couple days that Ping had been trained in London, which revealed why she spoke nearly perfect English. She had majored in music and was an able pianist. In her spare time she taught piano to others where she lived.

"Ping?" Allen inquired one morning. "What does your name mean?" "My mother said it means 'peaceful'," she replied.

Allen thought how fitting this was for her. She seemed like the perfect example of a person who desired that everyone love one another. She certainly brought peace to his isolated room each day she came.

Even though Allen was stronger Dr. Rasmussen had kept the pilot in isolation so that the word would not get out about him. Dr. Malin feared being shut down by some of the anti-American forces not far from the clinic.

Dr. Malin was glad that he had kept Allen in isolation when later that month the newspapers of that area, in opposition to the United Nations forces, published the news than an American Air Force pilot had left his squadron and flown into their territory for refuge.

The propaganda spread to the area was that Lieutenant Allen Livingston had given up his allegiance to the United States. This, of course, was untrue, but lies used to brainwash the people against the enemy were not uncommon.

Allen heard he had been court-marshaled and his rank taken away by the Commandant. Feeling rejected by his country he began to isolate himself from the others as misery settled in.

Ling, becoming a good friend to Allen, placed a scripture verse on

Page 76

the breakfast tray he brought every morning. He knew God was the only one to give Allen back his life, and Ling was relieved as Allen slowly began talking again.

The Early Days

Ping and Ling were glad that Allen was not so miserable anymore, and Ping enjoyed being able to bring a smile to his face. Being responsible for many patients, Ping arrived early to the clinic so she could spend more time in Allen's room. Allen always welcomed Ping's visits and missed her uplifting demeanor when she was absent a day or two.

"You are early today." Allen greeted Ping with a smile.

"Yes, I need to leave by mid-day, so I got here before many woke," Ping replied.

"Do you live near the clinic?" Allen inquired.

"No, I live in a neighboring town," she answered.

Allen pushed further, "Do you have a family?"

"I have two sisters, but no brothers," was her reply.

Allen was disappointed by Ping's short answers. He could tell she was of a higher caste because of her clothes, training, and academic abilities. He would have liked more information, but would not push her to share.

"I know you must go, but would you do me a favor before you leave?" he requested.

With caution she responded, "It depends on what it is."

"I used to have a girlfriend back home that would always hold my hand, and often she would pat it with the other hand to assure me she wanted to see me again. It was always comforting to me," he said sadly. "If I am asking too much of you, say so, but if you pat my hand that will tell me you are coming again," he said meekly.

Ping thought for a moment before she walked toward Allen and took his hand. She patted it gently and said, "I cannot come tomorrow, but I will see you on the next day."

A ritual had begun between Allen and Ping.

Ling Kai, while making his rounds in the clinic stopped in Allen's room. Since Ling was getting better in English he always enjoyed sitting and conversing. Likewise, Allen enjoyed someone to talk to and especially welcomed the visit each day by Ling. He would never forget that Ling, Lang and Noi helped bring him out of the jungle, saving him from bleeding to death by getting him to the Friendship Mission as soon as they could.

Days had passed and Allen was beginning to reminisce his growing up days as he recuperated. Ling recognized Allen's quietness and asked, "What are you thinking about?"

Allen said, "I was thinking about when I was a small boy and my father worked for Dr. Henry Hardin."

Ling quickly said, "I remember you speaking of a blacksmith, but what is a blacksmith?"

Allen answered, "It is a person who makes or repairs broken parts from metal. It was during World War II and my father had to repair everything because there were no new cars or tractors made during that period. My dad could make just about anything and Dr. Hardin saw to it that he had the material necessary to fix the farm equipment since food production was needed at the time."

Ling Kai was a very inquisitive person and queried more about Allen's youth.

"I suppose your father was very influential to you?"

Allen thought a moment before he replied, "Yes, both my parents were, but next to them I suppose it was my Sunday school teacher that influenced me most. A Sunday school teacher is a person who teaches the Bible to boys and girls in a church."

"You forget I attended a church back in China. I had a teacher who taught me. Of course we did not call it Sunday school, but Bible study. Her name was Mrs. Wong. What was your teacher's name?" "Her name was Mom Long." Allen said.

"Mom Long was three-fourths American Indian, and she was very well versed in the Bible and truly believed it all. She was also our preacher's wife, and at the age of thirteen we felt she was as close to God as anybody could be. I always listened to her every word.

"She taught me values and respect for God and His church by giving to it," Allen continued.

"As a boy delivering the local newspapers to homes in the community, I collected eighteen dollars from my paper route. I put my one dollar and eighty cents tithe in my secret pocket so I could give it to my church the next Sunday as Mom Long had taught us," Allen remembered.

"The day after my collecting was Saturday, the traditional shopping day in my home town and people came from out in the country by buses to town. I thought I would help my parents out by buying my school clothes for the coming year. My first purchase was three pairs of blue jeans. Afterwards, I bought two shirts at another store. My money was nearly all gone, but as I walked in front of the local department store I saw a beautiful blue shirt with white poke-a-dots.

"The price at the base of the shirt told me I didn't have enough to buy it, unless I went to the secret pocket for the needed money. I went on for about a block, before I turned back to take a second look.

"As I turned to leave again, my feet seemed to head into the store, and I did what I knew was wrong. Yes, I purchased that blue poke-a-dotted shirt after taking twenty-three cents of God's money out of my secret pocket.

"The next day," Allen continued, "I entered Sunday school wearing that new shirt and a pair of the jeans I had purchased. My guilt was evident as I immediately asked Mom Long, 'God doesn't care if I use some of His money to get what I wanted does He?'

"Ling, after all these years I can still hear her reply. 'Yes, sir, He does care! Before this day is over, something will happen to that shirt.' Well, I didn't know she was also a prophetess!

"She invited all of her class to her house for an after church dinner. We boys headed for the field and a little creek grabbing all the small fish we could. Our shoes got wet, as did our jeans. When she rang the bell on her back porch calling us to dinner, we all began to run. One of the fellows said, 'It is closer to the house if we go through the field fenced in with barbed wire.' Ling, do I have to tell you what happened to the back of a blue poke-a-dotted shirt?

"From that day on, I never took anything I knew was God's. I was thirteen at this time even though I did not become a Christian until I was seventeen.

"I tithed four years before my salvation because my Sunday school teacher instilled in me that everything was created by God for our betterment," Allen declared.

"I believed it, because I believed what she believed. I was born in a sharecropper's log house with very little hope for a life beyond that area. I honestly believe that what she taught me as a lad, has caused me to do things and go places I would not have been given the opportunity had I not believed her. I am convinced that what we are, and how we teach, does influence lives. And Ling, Mom Long still continues to teach me. She was one of the most influential persons in my youth."

"Wow! She must have been a straight forward teacher," Ling burst out. "I'd love to hear more of your stories, but I have to get my other work done this morning. I'll be back."

Ling left there soaking in all that was said by Allen, yet not understanding everything. He knew he would have to think about it for a while and come back with any question he could not work out himself.

After an hour or so, Ling came back and sat down by Allen's bed with a big smile. "You know Lieutenant Livingston; you are giving me things to think about. I like to learn about new cultures, new religions, and new people. Tell me more about what you did when you were a boy," Ling asked with all sincerity.

Allen stopped his reading and looked up at Ling.

"I used to spend my summers at my grandparents in the country where they had a farm and raised cotton for a living. Most of the land was poor and had many rocks. I was required to pick up the rocks and throw them to the side of the field. That was hard work for a boy that lived in town, but I really enjoyed being out with my grandparents and doing what they asked.

"My grandmother had written me when I was 12 and invited me to spend the summer with them. She did this to all who had been born on the farm.

"My grandmother was from Scotland, and I can still see her sitting in an old homemade rocker combing her hair. I had no idea how long it was because she always kept it rolled up in a bun. I was surprised when I saw her pulling her hair through the comb because her hair was so long she was not able to reach the end. I found out that this was a weekly chore for her, but one she didn't seem to mind. It was time to her self.

"I would enjoy watching her sit, rock and sing. I remember one of her favorite lyrics: *'All my life long I had panted for a draft from some cool spring that I hoped would quench the burning that I felt so deep within.'*"

"Ling, you would have loved Grandma. She'd get to the end of the stanza, throw her hands up in the air, and with tears in her eyes she's shout praises to the lord with the chorus: *'Hallelujah, I have found Him, Oh, my soul so long had craved. Jesus satisfies my longing through His precious blood I'm saved."*

Allen had taken the time to reveal this portion of his life in a way he felt Ling would understand it easiest.

"You must have loved your elder parents a lot," Ling commented.

"Yes, my grandmother really had a lot of influence on me. In fact, she probably spanked me more than my mother. She made sure I was doing what she asked. She wanted me to live right."

Ling noticed that Allen was looking tired and knew he needed some rest.

"I better go and let you rest now. Thank you for sharing your life with me. May I come back tomorrow to talk more?"

"I'd love to share more with you," Allen answered as Ling quietly departed.

Ling Inquires Of The Allen's Church Life

The next day Ling showed up Allen's room with a list of questions.

"You are later than usual today," remarked Allen.

"Yes, I wanted to be with you last so I might stay longer and ask some questions. I enjoyed listening to you yesterday, and I didn't want to be interrupted by my duties. I hope you do not mind," admitted Ling.

"I don't mind at all. What is it that you want to know?" asked Allen.

"I have noticed on several occasions that you have been wheeled to the music room down the hall. What age were you when you learned to play the piano and other instruments?" Ling began.

"Well, Ling, I have had very little official training. I learned to play on my own. I simply learned to play by the sound of notes rather than by reading the music. In my country they often call that "playing by ear." My family and background, as I have shared, was of a humble beginning. However, I was lucky to have caring parents who attempted to direct both my sister and me into events that would better us. At times I wondered what would be the advantage or significance of some of those things, but I'm slowly learning why they were important to my life.

"For instance, one such event was a gospel music school that I attended every year at our church. Little did I know the likes of some of those men would become famous as time rewarded them.

"One of my most well known teachers was Marvin P. Dalton. He wrote two songs that fill churches throughout my country: 'O, What a

Savior' and 'Looking for a City.'

"Another teacher was Luther G. Presley. He lived near my home town and no one would have dreamed that local boy along with Virgil O. Stamps would compose a famous melody in 1937 that would be sung around the English speaking world. He's the one that penned the immortal lyrics to 'When the Saints Go Marching In.'

"Today anyone can sing a few lines or hum a few bars of that melody. An article in one of our newspapers once described Luther Presley as the state's most prolific songwriter. He has composed the music or written the lyrics to hundreds of gospel songs!

"And you know, Ling, he was not even as old as you are when he started to write songs of praise because of his faith. Mr. Presley grew up with religious music at a Free Will Baptist Church. At fourteen he attended his first music school and began directing the church choir. He wrote his first song, 'Gladly Sing,' when he was seventeen. My favorite song of his is 'I'd Rather Have Jesus.' He wrote that after he had studied the parable of the rich man in the twelfth chapter of Luke.

"I figured if he could do it in his youth, so could I. That's when I decided to start learning how to play the piano and guitar, my two favorite instruments," declared Allen.

"I also remember well my last teacher. He was Albert E. Brumley. In 1932 his song 'I'll Fly Away' was published. Since then Mr. Brumley has written hundreds of gospel and sentimental songs. His songs emulate country settings, ordinary country religion, simplicity and values.

"His education was little and his occupations have consisted of being a cotton farmer, piano tuner, singing school teacher, and grocery store clerk. He had such a humble life like me. He inspired me to continue learning music," Allen explained as he completed his brief history lesson.

"I must tell you, Ling, this part of my past has been only a reflection of my present, as well as the mirror of God's plan for me in the future."

"I'm not sure I understand what you are meaning," replied Ling.

"I did not realize, at the time, that these men were not only giving me something to live with, but they also gave me something to die with. The third verse of Marvin Dalton's famous song 'O What a Savior' says it best:

Death's chilly waters I'll soon be crossing. His hand will lead me safe o're. I'll join the chorus in that great city, and sing up there forever more."

As Allen sang, Ling listened closely and then hastened to ask, "Is there more? Sing all of it."

Allen gladly continued with the chorus:

"*O what a Savior, O Hallelujah, His heart was broken on Calvary. His hands were nail scarred. His side was riven. He gave his life-blood for even me.*"

Tears had risen in Allen's eyes as he concluded the song.

"Open your Bible, Ling, and read Psalm 40:3 to me," pleaded Allen.

"*And He hath put a new song in my mouth, even praise unto our God: many shall see it, and fear, and shall trust in the Lord,*" read Ling in his broken English.

"Ling, these songs of my youth are now aiding me during my recuperation. To hum and sing these songs blesses me when I am discouraged and sad," Allen confessed.

"I now appreciate the summers and Sunday afternoons visiting churches for gospel sings. These events were so much a part of my growing up years and are now such a part of my adult life. The Word in song is certainly sustaining," finished Allen.

"My youth," Ling shared, "was much like yours with music. Our music was not as fast. I am learning to like your music beat," laughed Ling.

What About The School Days?

Allen could hardly sleep that night because of the emotions his discussion with Ling had created. It had been so long since he had even thought about his early days, and now he had so many memories coming back to him. These discussions helped Allen during his recovery period, and they were also building a bond with his new friend, Ling.

Allen stayed out of sight most of the time since he was in a foreign country with little chance of getting out without being arrested. His only advantage was that the area was so ravaged by war. With three or four factional groups fighting to control the area, the clinic was left alone.

Ling and Dr. Malin had both told Allen of the danger that existed within a few miles. Most of the people were at war with each other, however, and knew Dr. Malin had a humanitarian compound and medical clinic. The doctor had friends on at least two of the warring sides, but kept a neutral stand. With these relationships and the fear that they may need the clinic themselves in the future, there seemed to be no interest by any of the groups to destroy the compound and clinic.

The sun had not been up long when Ling brought Allen his breakfast.

"I'm looking forward to listening to your life's story again today. Do you feel up to it?" Ling asked.

Allen affirmed Ling's desire and they set a time for later in the day when they could talk uninterrupted. The hour finally arrived and Ling burst into the room with a desire to get right to the questions he had planned to ask.

"Did you enjoy your high school?" Ling began.

"Not really. I barely even made it to graduation!" Allen reluctantly admitted.

"What happened?"

"After a week of absence from school because of a basketball tournament, I returned knowing I had two assignments due in my last class of the day. With a library session before that class, I hurried to finish the assignments. Nothing seemed to satisfy me, so I went to a literature book and began to do what I shouldn't. I copied someone else's stories. I turned in both assignments with great merriment. I believed the teacher would see just how smart I was," Allen revealed.

"Well, the next afternoon I received a different feeling when the teacher said, 'Allen, I want to see you after class.'

"I had no idea why she wanted to see me at that point, but moments later found out why. She slid one of the stories onto my desk and said, 'I couldn't believe you would do this! Of all the boys in my class, you! You! I am so hurt and disappointed in you!'

"By then I was feeling very low. I wilted entirely when she said, 'I don't remember who wrote this, but I know it wasn't you. I read this more than 25 years ago when I was in college. I cannot accept this assignment.'

"Needless to say, my parents were not too happy with me either," Allen admitted. "In my high school, the disciplinary consequence for this type behavior was a week's expulsion. I had to check out with the principal and knew I would not get credit for anything missed that week.

"Tuesday night came, and I knew a lot of young people were going to a small church about fifteen miles away where a young preacher was holding a revival. I wasn't too interest in a revival, but I did have some interest in a cute blond that would be there. I had heard she had a liking for me, so my desire to go to that revival was increased." Allen winked at Ling who sat laughing and waving his hand for Allen to continue.

"The preaching style of this preacher was different, and he got my attention early on. He was young, but he immediately convinced me that he believed everything he was talking about. Occasionally I would look over at the girl and smile. She was flirting back as well, but these glances didn't happen very often. The preacher was actually interesting, and by the conclusion of his sermon I was ready to make a decision.

"I had never felt so convicted inside, and I was ready to burst into tears. I knew I was guilty and responsible for my sins. He made this so plain to me. I went forward to the altar and received Jesus along with most of the other visiting teens," Allen said in a rejoicing manner.

When Allen hesitated in his storytelling, Ling prompted, "But that isn't the end of the story is it? What happened after that?"

"The next Monday, that same school teacher said she wanted me to stay after class again. 'O, no!' I had said to myself. 'She found the other one!'

"To my surprise she gave me the news that I would not fail her class. She said, 'Some of the students told me you made a decision to change you ways last week. Well, I am going to forgive you also, but this time you will have to write something for me that is original.'

"I thanked her, and my Lord, that I would not be an embarrassment to my family, myself, and my Savior.

"Since I needed something I alone wrote, I began to compose a poem. I still have that little poem, that I turned into a teacher who had enough belief in me to give me a second opportunity, memorized. I'll just bet that you want to hear it," joked Allen.

"You know that I do," answered Ling.

"Keep going."

"The poem was entitled, 'The Bible.' Here is how it goes:"

I know of a book that is wonderful to me,
It is one I as a Christian always like to see.
It is a glorious book so rich and so free,
And it tells me stories on how I can be me.
This book tells me stories of the young and the old,
It tells me how to live my life and enriches my soul.
Many men with their understanding and instinct,
Are not really as smart as some people may think,
For men in their greatness have said, 'It's not liable,'
Yet they in their smartness don't understand all the Bible."

"Wow," Ling said. "That is really good for a new Christian to write. I have been a Christian for many years, but I'm not sure I could have explained it so well. How did your teacher like it?"

"That poem not only gave me an 'A', but the ability to graduate. I could have never gone to college had it not been for a teacher who cared."

"What did you study when you went to college?" Ling questioned. "I assumed that you were always a military man."

"No, Ling. It was only a few weeks later, while I was still a high school senior, that I pledged to serve the Lord as a minister," confessed Allen. "It was only a short time until our senior class trip, and I was asked to speak. It was my first attempt before my peers, and it was hard, but I was glad to be asked. I was excited to enter Dexter College just a couple months later and begin my study for the ministry."

As Allen finished this part of his life's story, Ping, running late due to some delays at home, entered Allen's room. She had remembered her promise to return, and she made sure to see him today.

"I better get to work, Allen, but I want to know what happened with you in college," said Ling. "I'll be leaving you in good hands now."

As Ling left the room, Ping approached the chair Allen occupied. "I hope you don't mind my eaves-dropping, but I heard the beautiful story you told Ling of how you got out of high school. Was the girl you went to see at the revival very pretty?"

Allen was quite taken aback by this question from Ping. Answering her honestly he said, "Yes. She had long blond hair and a beautiful complexion. And, she had a great smile." "Was she as pretty as me?" Ping inquired.

Allen thought for a moment longer before he answered. He wasn't sure what Ping was seeking from him. "I was just a young man and certainly not very mature. When she didn't come forward with the other teens and me to accept Jesus, my interest in her seemed to leave me. Beauty is more than a face, so I don't think I could ever compare her with you."

This was the answer Ping wanted, but she felt embarrassed to have asked.

Allen could sense her discomfort and continued with a sincere response, "I know of no one as beautiful as you are! Your beauty goes beyond face and body."

Ping's warm smile brightened the whole room as she took Allen by the hand and patted it. This simple gesture was her quiet way of promising to see him again.

As Ping left without saying another word, Allen's thoughts, spurred by his conversation with Ling, turned to his four years at DexterCollege. He had been very serious about his study for the ministry, and he had shown real improvement in his grades.

He reminisced about playing basketball in the intramurals and being selected to the All-Star team. Those pleasant days seemed so long ago now. He had loved and lost, and the ministry he had studied so hard to achieve had never come to pass either. Now he lived with the lie by a flying partner governing his future.

The Difficult Breakup

Ling was noticing how much anger Allen lost each day as he told his life's story. Today, however, as he entered Allen's room he could sense that Allen was feeling a little down.

"You are sad today, my friend?" Ling questioned.

"I have been thinking about the next part of my story to you. Yes, there is heartache in this next chapter." Allen answered.

"Do you still want to continue sharing with me?"

"Yes, but do you think you could wheel me outside to talk today? The bright sunshine would be nice," suggested Allen.

After Ling had Allen settled in a private area of the compound's flower garden, Allen began.

"I was just about ready to graduate, and I thought my future was laid perfectly out in front of me. I had been dating a girl named Helen Mabrey for two years and our relationship had been very enjoyable. Helen was outgoing but somewhat flirtatious. There were a few times that I had felt uncomfortable being with her on our dates because she would often hang around the other boys as much as she would me. I'll admit that on several occasions I questioned if she would make a good minister's wife, but she was so much fun to be around, and she was very pretty. I just assumed that she was just the right girl who would be willing to share my life's work."

"It did not happen that way?" Ling questioned.

"No. On the way to a game one night, Helen asked me to stop the car. She wouldn't look at me, but rather looked out the window as she began to talk. She said, 'Allen, I don't want to be a minister's wife. These have been two of the most fun years I have ever had. You are in the center of everything and most of the time the life of the party, but you are going into something I am not sure I want to share.'

"This was such a blow to me. For the first time in my life I remember being speechless. I had been saddened before, but this was breaking my heart. I can remember how the tears filled my eyes, but I held back the weeping. I finally suggested we go home, and she readily agreed.

"When we got to her house I slowly got out of the car to open her door. She still wouldn't look me in the eyes as she said, 'You do not have to walk me to the door. I would rather you wouldn't.'

"Have you ever loved someone, Ling?"

"There was a girl I think I could have had a future with, but I had to leave her when my brothers and I left our country. I never got to say goodbye to her." Ling answered. "I believe I can understand your loss."

The two friends sat in silence for a while. Allen finally decided to continue.

"The next day was hard for me to return to the college. I stopped at the student center where I usually had a cup of coffee with a couple buddies, and I noticed they were somewhat subdued. I could tell they were uncomfortable being with me. Finally one of them blurted out, 'It's all over campus that you and Helen have broken up. Is this true?'

"My eyes immediately filled with the tears that didn't seem to end. I explained to them how she didn't want the life of a minister's wife. My friends were ministerial students as well and they looked at each other before one spoke. It was hard to hear what he had to say, but somehow I knew my friend was telling me the truth. He said, 'We know this is hard for you, but too many ministers are pulled down by a non-compatible wife. So it is really better this happen now don't you think?'

"I wasn't ready yet to agree, so I got up to leave the center. My friends chose to leave with me. They walked one on either side of me to show their friendship during this hard time. I can still remember how they supported me over the next few weeks.

"College just wasn't the same anymore. Helen and I had been inseparable and suddenly we never even saw each other. I guess she was avoiding me. I must admit that at the time I wasn't sure how I would respond to her if I did run into her.

"My classes didn't seem the same either. They didn't hold my interest in the same way, and my grades even began to suffer. I had a professor stop me and ask what was bothering me, but I told him it was a personal problem that I needed to work out on my own.

"Sometimes, Ling, especially in the quiet of night, I question the Lord as to why I am stuck with another serious personal problem. I feel that same heartbreak all over again, only this time it comes from my country."

Ling tried to comfort Allen. "The Lord is the best one to question about that. He knows the reason this has all happened. I wish I had better words like your friend in college."

As Allen sat back in his chair he let out a deep sigh, "Ling, your friendship right now is the best thing I have in my life. I am very thankful for you."

Ling, having started pushing Allen back, reached out and patted his friend's shoulder. "You obviously made it through that time in your life. I know you are too tired now to continue the story, but as you rest this afternoon, remember that you can make it through this time too."

It Was A Very Sad Day

As Allen lay in bed resting he thought of how his college career had ended. The final grades had been mailed and he was graduating, but not with the kind of excitement he once had. He knew Helen would be just a few people behind him in the processional, and thoughts of their lost relationship still weighed heavy on his heart.

The day of graduation was rather bittersweet for Allen. He sat waiting for his close friend, Aaron Lybarger, to deliver the valedictorian address.

The dean of the college introduced Aaron who came to the podium with his address notes by his side. He laid the papers down neatly and put his hands on both sides of the podium. He stood there for a moment to relax and gain his composure. Then he began in a clear and confident voice.

"It's graduation! Can you believe it?

"Today, in just a few minutes, you and I will receive our diplomas and be recognized for our ability to complete the courses of study.

"I want you to know that you do not become a success today. You are only being recognized as successful today.

"Today is the end of one era in our lives and the beginning of a new one. It is important that as we start this new journey we realize how we live from this point on will determine whether or not we continue to be successful."

Aaron was an excellent speaker, and the contents of his message weighed heavily on Allen.

"If you want to accomplish, you have to recognize that you cannot rely upon your grade point average, your diploma, or any titles or positions.

"If you want to be successful you have to work at it.

"You never arrive.

"You can only strive.

"The Bible says that we have to strive to bear fruit. We have to be fruitful and productive. It takes a lot of work to be truly productive. Good intentions alone will not get you there.

"You know what I am talking about, right?

"Good intentions are just that – good intentions! To be effective it takes work. It takes effort. Proverbs 13:4 says, *'The soul of the sluggard desireth, and hath nothing: but the soul of the diligent shall be made fat.'*

"Success is not measured by what we have; it is measured by what we do to help others. Proverbs 11:25 says, *'The liberal soul shall be made fat: and he that watereth shall be watered also himself.'* And in Proverbs 11:3, *'The integrity of the upright shall guide them: but the perverseness of transgressors shall destroy them.'*

"You cannot be successful without integrity. When you are honest, people will trust you. When you are honest with people, you gain their trust and their respect. When you are honest with God, you gain His trust and favor. You will not be a success if you are not honest with yourself, God, and others.

"To be successful you have to be willing to put others first. Why? Because the more you do for others the more it comes back to you.

"The most direct way to the top is from the bottom.

"To start being content try the following: refuse to compare yourself to others, give away something you value a lot, and choose to live on less than you are comfortable with rather than more than you make.

"Remember, God gives you what you have. Always be content with what you have, but never with what you are.

"Without Jesus you might attain some great things, but they will only last a lifetime. With Jesus you can be productive for an eternity!

"If you desire to live a successful life let me encourage you to start by making a commitment to God. Start by entering into a relationship with the God who made you. Ask Him to forgive you for the things you have done wrong and ask Him to be the leader of your life."

Aaron had addressed his peers with fervor and sincerity. The closing of his speech invited the class to make a decision. Everyone sat quietly and the school leaders on the platform remained seated. They seemed to be stunned by the forcefulness and content of the message.

Aaron had gotten to the point from the start. It seemed to Allen as if he was the only one in the listening audience. He thought over and over that Aaron was talking right straight to him, challenging him to rise above the hurt and do what he had planned to do with his life.

As each graduate marched across the stage and received their diploma, Allen caught the eye of Helen and nodded to her. As they were seated he said, "Well, we made it this far." She smiled agreeably.

When the ceremony was over Allen and Helen moved toward each other. When they met she looked at him and spoke, "Allen, I am so sorry I hurt you. I want the best for you, and I hope everything works out for your life. I've been wanting to tell you, before the word gets around, that I am dating Phillip Jones now. He is very nice. Are you seeing anyone now?"

Allen answered in the negative and began to move away from Helen as he said, "Perhaps we will meet again sometime."

This news about Phillip reopened the wounds in Allen's heart. He still loved Helen, and Phillip was not at all what he would have wished for her. Phillip had a reputation for not respecting girls and he drank heavily.

As Allen lay in his bed thinking of how this new relationship for Helen caused her to leave her church and move in with Phillip his dinner tray arrived. He welcomed the distraction as he could feel the old feelings of sadness begin to overwhelm him.

Her Death Forced A New Beginning

After graduating college Allen had continued to be disillusioned about entering the ministry and began to look for something else to do. Somehow he thought God had tested him, and he failed to the point the Lord had removed the call. This wore on Allen's mind because he had been so excited about being a minister, but now was puzzled.

Allen's parents noticed a great change in him, and they were greatly concerned about how remote he was acting. They knew of Helen's wrong doing and how it was affecting him.

One day Martha Livingston opened the local newspaper and leaping out to her on the front page of the Log Cabin Democrat was a photo of the crash and headline that read, "Phillip Jones and Helen Mabrey Killed in a Head-on Collision." As she read down the story she learned that they had both been drinking and crossed the center line, running into an oncoming car. The driver, wife, and three children in the other car were also killed.

Martha Livingston was stunned by the article and sat in a chair at the kitchen table and began to reread the story. She wondered how this would further affect Allen. She loved him deeply and they were very close, but lately Allen had been pulling away from her, and she dreaded how this news may be taken by him.

When her husband, David, came in from work she showed him the paper. They both were hardly able to say anything and so fell to their knees and silently prayed together. They were both very religious and had raised their children to trust God in everything, but they knew this would be devastating to Allen. They had seen the love that Allen had for Helen, and they had seen his heart broken when the relationship ended.

A couple hours later Allen came in and noticed right away something was wrong. His parents were not their jovial selves, and they both kept looking at him with such sympathy.

"What's wrong?" he finally asked.

"We have bad news Allen. We just don't know how to tell you," his mother said with tears beginning to pool in her eyes.

"It can't be that bad. I can take it!" he said.

She opened the paper, and Allen spotted the photo and headline immediately. With only a few lines of reading he rushed to his room and began to cry. He was broken more than he wanted to show in front of his parents. He fell to his knees and sobbed.

"If I could have just . . . If she would have just . . .

"Why did she make the wrong decisions? Look what it has cost her. She was only twenty-one years old. And Phillip. The other family."

Allen continued his broken thought pattern as great remorse began to settle on him. He finally cried out, "Oh, God. My God!"

When he was able to gather himself emotionally, he returned to his family in the sitting room. "Do you think I drove her to this?" He offered the question to no one in particular.

Allen's mother, in her remarkable wisdom, said, "She is the one who knew what she wanted. Now she has paid the price for the wrong choice. No, you did not drive her to this."

The Livingston's phone began to ring with words of comfort from many friends, but Allen was not easily convinced that he was not responsible for some of what had happened.

The next day Allen ran into Donald Brogan, one of his high school classmates. Donald was obviously in a jolly mood and excitedly said, "I just joined the Air Force. Why don't you join the action and come with me?"

With only a brief thought as to what he was saying, Allen asked Donald where the recruiter's office was and immediately headed that direction.

After the presentation Allen began to think seriously about enlisting. He believed that this may be what he would like to do. The ministry was obviously not going to work out. "I think getting away from here might be exactly what I need. Maybe a new course of action would help me," he thought to himself.

That night he announced to his parents what he was considering. His father, a veteran himself, said, "Son, if that is what you want, I will stand with you."

His mother was not as affirmative and began to cry. "I just hope you know what you are doing. Please promise that you will pray about this decision. You have been hurt so much lately. It is so far away from what you said God was calling you to do. I don't want you out of His will, and I know you don't want that either. But if you do choose to sign up, I want you to know I will pray for you daily."

The next day Allen walked back into the recruiter's office. The recruiter walked from around his desk while reaching for Allen's hand and said, "I knew you would come back. I already have the papers prepared. Just sign right here."

His Life's Detour

Allen had gone home from the recruiter's office and called Donald to let him know that he had joined the Air Force too. "I am glad you called and let me know you joined. Perhaps we can get together and make plans for our departure. It sounds as if we will be traveling to basic training on the same day."

"Are you physically ready for basic training?" Allen asked.

"I found some information in the packet about the shape we should be in. I don't suppose you have had time to read yours yet, but let me tell you what it suggests. It says, 'The best thing you can do to be ready is to prepare yourself in advance. Getting an early start on physical conditioning is among the most important steps you can take to be successful. Three days of aerobic running alternated with three days of muscular fitness exercises. All sessions are preceded by pre-exercise limbering and end with a series of post-exercise stretches.' I am in pretty good shape, but just the thought of all the running, exercising, and stretching makes me tired already."

"Me, too!" Allen replied.

The two fellows began to meet at the school track to run on a regular basis and work out in the gym. Their weight dropped a few pounds, and they toned their muscles greatly.

They had not seen each other much during the four years Allen had been in college. Allen wasn't even aware that Donald had been attending the University of Arkansas at Little Rock during that same period. As they trained each day, they renewed and strengthened their friendship. They were not only in strong physical health, but they were fast becoming mental support for each other.

The day of departure came and the two friends boarded the bus, along with other fellows from their area that were headed to

Lackland Air Force Base in San Antonio, Texas.

It was a long trip from Conway, but the excitement, along with some fears, existed in the conversations of nearly every fellow. Some tried to hide this by expressing their manliness, but others were honest about it. For most it was the first time away from their parents, and many wondered if they could meet up to the requirements set by the officers at the base.

When the bus arrived inside the base they were advised of where they would bunk and what would happen the first few days.

The first time the group met in formation Sergeant Oliver Southard was introduced. "Gentlemen, welcome to Lackland. Some of you will hate it here, and some of you who believe in what we do will love it. It is up to you to decide. We are an Air Force Basic Military Training post for all enlisted people entering the Air Force, Air Force Reserve and Air National Guard. We are sometimes called the 'Gateway to the Air Force.'

"You will be among approximately 35,000 Airmen trained here this year. Following graduation you may go on to technical training at Lackland or elsewhere for your first Air Force assignment. Many thousands of Airmen have completed training here since the base opened in 1946," he concluded.

The weeks passed quickly for Livingston and Brogan. They were both college graduates so the classroom work was easily learned and having prepared physically beforehand made the extensive physical training less strenuous. Some of the other men learned basic training was harder than they thought, and many of them began to hate their decision, but feared the consequence if they said anything.

Finally the graduation from basic came and there was much rejoicing. It was the first time families could visit, so Livingston's folks had come, and the time spent with them after the commencement was pleasant.

Allen's mother was the first to reach him. Hugging him tightly she said, "Congratulations! We are so proud of you, but has this brought you peace?"

Mr. Livingston, stepping in to shake Allen's hand, stopped his wife before she went further saying, "Now, Mom, this is not the time for bringing that up."

As Allen released his dad's hand he grinned and replied, "I thought you might ask this while you were here, so let's just get it out of the way. I am still working through it."

"We have been so worried about you and have prayed for you every day," his dad added.

"Thank you. I'm sure it probably helped me more than I am aware. Brogan and I have found a community church here in San Antonio, and we have begun to get help for many of our problems. In fact, just yesterday we signed up to meet regularly with the pastor for Bible reading and prayer," stated Allen.

One of the training officers, Captain Joseph Shipney, had watched and observed Livingston and Brogan. He approached them before the next training assignments were issued. "Fellows, upon recommendations from Sergeant Southard, I have been watching your performance. He seemed very impressed with your physical and leadership abilities, and I have to agree with him. You are more talented than most, and I would like to assign you to the next class at Officer Candidate School. After your completion you can celebrate your commission as Second Lieutenants in the United States Air Force."

Livingston and Brogan looked at each and quickly agreed that Officer Candidate School would be a challenge they would like to undertake.

"The Officer Candidate School produces world-class officers of character who possess the American warrior ethos, embody the Air Force Core Values, and become better prepared to lead other

Airmen," stated Captain Shipney. "The Basic Officer program consists of twelve weeks of military instruction for college graduates leading to your commissions. The goal of this training is to instill high standards of conduct and provide officer candidates with the essential military knowledge and skills needed for effective performance as Air Force Leaders.

"You will have the opportunity after Officer Candidate School to pursue other technical specialties that will include pilot training, navigation, air battle management, space and missile operations, and several other support career fields.

"Once you complete all school requirements you will be given the oath of office and commissioned on extended active duty in the Air Force."

Livingston and Brogan said instantly, "I want to be a pilot."

Captain Shipney finished explaining, "The Officer Candidate School's motto *'Always with Honor'* is reflected in the school's honor code: *'We will not lie, steal or cheat, nor tolerate among us anyone who does.'* The code is a standard of personal conduct for each officer trainee. Officer Candidate School expects each graduate to adopt the code as the ethical standard maintained throughout their Air Force careers. After watching you two men, I believe you will have no problems with that."

There was a high expectancy set by the officers in charge at the school, and while the first few weeks were tough for both Livingston and Brogan, they were very excited about the prospect of training as a pilot and worked hard to complete their class goals. Many of the classes involved their role in leadership, and both men were encouraged as the teachings came naturally to them.

Many of the other class members were conscious of Livingston and Brogan's abilities, so gravitated toward them and developed close friendships. The officers leading the program took into consideration all they witnessed and put in a high recommendation for the two men to continue into the pilot training program.

Livingston and Brogan were both excited to hear the Post Commander introduce them as Lieutenant Allen Livingston and Lieutenant Donald Brogan. They knew they could now continue to pursue their goal of entering pilot training school.

Due to the recommendations of the officers, they were quickly accepted into the school and their exuberant shouts of joy could be heard all over the barracks.

He Enters Pilot Training

It had been fortunate that both previous programs had been in San Antonio. Pilot training would be at Kelly Air Force Base, the oldest continuously operating flight base in the United States Air Force. It was located at the southwestern edge of the city.

Captain Benjamin Foulois, the "Father of Military Aviation," selected the site in November 1916 to expand the activities of the fledgling Aviation Section of the United States Army Signal Corps from Fort Sam Houston. The new airfield was named for Lieutenant George E. Kelly, who was killed in a crash at Fort Sam Houston on May 10, 1911. He was the first American military aviator to lose his life while piloting a military aircraft.

Lieutenants Livingston and Brogan grew with pride when they learned that at some point of their training many of the early leaders of the Air Force passed through Kelly Field. The list included the Air Force Chiefs of Staff Carl "Tooey" Spaatz, Hoyt Vandenberg, and Curtis LeMay. Charles Lindbergh earned his wings at Kelly Field as did the famous "Flying Tiger" Claire Lee Chennault.

Kelly maintained such aircrafts as the B-29, B-36, B-47 and B-58 bombers, numerous types of fighters including the F-102 and F-105, and various cargo planes. Livingston and Brogan were assigned to train in the F-105 fighters.

As their training advanced they met and became more acquainted with future members of their squadron. Their leader would be Colonel Joe Glenn with other members: Lieutenant Sam Cunningham, Lieutenant Robert Grissom, and Captain Jeff Nichols.

Colonel Joe Glenn was a career pilot and had grown up in California. He was divorced and never got to see his daughter. He had good leadership skills, but at times was easily influenced by vocal opponents.

Captain Jeff Nichols, also a career pilot, was actually a better leader than Glenn, but lacked the years of active duty. He was a family man with a lovely wife and a set of twin girls. The Nichols' family was from College Park, Georgia, and still had sweet southern accents when they spoke.

Lieutenant Robert Grissom was from Knob Lick, Missouri. He had lived in many areas of the state as his father got transferred many times within their denomination. He was still single, but had a high school sweetheart back home.

Lieutenant Sam Cunningham had a bitter spirit and didn't care much for Christians. He kept his personal life to himself. His fellow squadron members learned only that he was from Oklahoma and had no parents or family that he cared to talk about.

Livingston learned quickly that Cunningham was a coarse fellow who didn't seem to be a team player. He approached Cunningham for their first meeting and offered a salute and hand of greeting, "It is a privilege to serve with you," Livingston stated.

Cunningham's answer stunned Livingston as he caustically responded, "I hear you are some kind of a do-gooder and Holy-Joe. Well, I would rather serve with any other type person than you!"

Colonel Glenn heard Lieutenant Cunningham's remarks and reprimanded him on the spot, "Lieutenant, this is a team where all of us have been chosen due to our abilities and leadership. I never want to hear that kind of talk again in this unit."

***

Livingston, Brogan, and Grissom had become close friends, but missed people outside the military community. Since all three were believers they sought for fellowship in a local church. They had found a very friendly church just a few miles out of town and were fortunate to be able to catch a bus from their base in order to attend every service they were available for.

They really liked Pastor Bob Graham, not only for his friendliness toward them, but his messages were Biblical and very challenging. Due to Lieutenant Cunningham's recent remarks the three newly assigned officers sought the pastor's advice in regards to how to cope with him.

Pastor Graham started by saying, "I do not know the man, but I do know the traits of that type. I believe your success in dealing with your friend is in how you respond as Christians.

"The Bible tells us in Ephesians 3: 20-21, *'Now unto him that is able to do exceeding abundantly above all that we ask or think, according to the power that works in us, Unto him be glory in the church by Christ Jesus throughout all ages, world without end. Amen.'*

"It appears Lieutenant Cunningham is struggling for success in the wrong way. Gentlemen, success is not found in riches, it is not found in fame, nor is it found in power. Success is only found in Christ Jesus. And I will suggest that success is found in attitude.

"When things happen to us in life, our attitude determines how we will respond. In other words, reaction will create our action.

"When I was in the Navy visiting Hong Kong, I walked through the downtown streets looking at all the different little shops. I came across a tattoo shop and noticed one that read 'Born to Lose.' I asked the store owner, 'Does anyone really ever buy that tattoo?' The store owner replied, 'Yes, sometimes, but before tattoo on skin, tattoo on mind.'

"Too many people have a loser attitude that shows up in how they live their lives. I think Philippians 2:5 says it well, *'Let this mind be in you which was also in Christ Jesus.'* In other words, have the attitude of Christ.

"Secondly belief and faith in God causes men to do great things, therefore, success comes from commitment. You must be committed to Christ.

"And there you have the ABC's of successful living: Attitude, Belief, and Commitment," concluded the pastor.

The three officers were overwhelmed by the power of his words. They were pointed at the truth and they could tell he believed it with his whole heart.

"This was just like the lesson preached by my friend in his valediction address," Livingston stated. "It was just what I needed to hear again."

The three buddies returned to the base and reread the passages the pastor had suggested, knowing they would be seeing Lieutenant Cunningham the next day.

The Airmen's Pledge

As the squadron assembled, Colonel Glenn introduced them to the plane they would begin to fly. "Gentlemen, behind me is the F-105. It has served on active duty with the U.S. Air Force for many years, much longer than most of its contemporaries. It is commonly called the Republic F-105 Thunderchief and is a supersonic fighter-bomber used in the specialized suppression of enemy air defenses and very able in its role against surface-to-air missile sites.

"Note the F-105 is armed with missiles and a M61A1 Vulcan 20mm cannon gun capable of firing 6,600 rounds per minute. Its operation is based upon the principle used in the rapid-firing gun invented by Richard J. Gatling in the 1860s. It has six rotating barrels, firing one at a time, which permits a high rate of fire while at the same time reducing the problem of barrel wear and heat generation.

"Gentlemen it was first flown in 1955 and the Thunderchief entered service in 1958 after additional improvements. It is the largest single-engine fighter ever employed by the USAF to date and the single-seat F-105 is adapted to deliver a greater bomb load than the four-engined, 10-man strategic bombers of World War II like the B-17 and B-24.

"You will be in control of one of these great planes," He announced.

In his concluding remarks Colonel Glenn commanded, "Fellows this is your plane: baby it, keep it clean, and advise your ground crew if something isn't working right."

Every man, with some apprehension, followed the Colonel to the aircraft assigned him. "The slower plane you trained in is now behind you. This is the day for the big show," the Colonel added.

As the planes taxied out to the runway at Kelly, each man looked at all the instruments to review what all were for.

Colonel Glenn said on his takeoff, "Fellows, we will start slow, and within a few minutes you will begin to see the power of this bird.

There's no time for carelessness. Just listen to me."

Livingston's turn came next, and he pushed the elevators to the proper position. As he pulled the throttle, the G's were obvious as the sound and the power of this flying machine headed upward. "This is awesome!" he shouted with a tint of fear.

All were finally airborne, and the Colonel began to call for the formation. "Now your real training has begun," he said.

Weeks of intense training began paying off. The men were more confident in their flying and camaraderie was usually present. Cunningham didn't come around Livingston when he was reading the Bible and was still reluctant to socialize much with any in the squadron.

Livingston, Brogan, and Grissom had discussed Cunningham's demeanor and Lieutenant Grissom, a minister's son, said, "I believe, just as Pastor Graham suggested, that Cunningham's attitude is based on some hurt he had in the past. A hurt probably inflicted by a Christian."

On one of the many training flights the squadron landed at Wright-Patterson Air Force Base near Dayton, Ohio. "There will be enough time for anyone who wants to visit the famous Air Force museum to do so," Colonel Glenn advised.

Livingston, Brogan, and Captain Nichols agreed they would like to visit the museum. They were the only ones who had not been there before. They were interested in the history of flying and knew they would find every type plane or flying machine imaginable.

More than one hundred planes from the earliest Wright reproduction to the fast jets of the present time were inside or around the huge building. They had visited other aeronautical centers on other occasions, but on this trip they discovered something under the wing of a huge B36. It was a B29 Super Fortress that had a famous history, and they were eager to learn more about it.

Livingston, who had spent many hours studying aviation history, burst out to his friends, "Fellows, many Super Fortresses were flown during World War II, but this one is truly famous. This one is named the 'Bockscar,' and it gained its fame from dropping the second atom bomb on Japan on August 9, 1945.

"The first atom bomb had been dropped three days earlier on Hiroshima killing 92,000, but this plane was used to kill 40,000 more Japanese on Nagasaki. That bombing brought the conclusion of World War II just one day later on August 10. Fellows, that day represented two celebrations. The war's end and my eighth birthday," Livingston concluded.

Captain Nichols advised the other two pilots that it was time for them to return back to Kelly Air Force Base. Shortly, Dayton was a small geographical dot as the planes roared heading back toward their home base.

Then it was back to the completion of studies required to graduate. The excitement was growing among the squadron and their other peers. They knew that in just a few days they would receive their wings.

Kelly Field was filled with family and friends that had come to see the award given to each airman finishing the training. The day's weather was warm with a nice breeze blowing. As the visitors finished taking the seats provided for them, the Air Force brass marched to the platform built for the occasion.

The barracks had been buzzing as each man polished his shoes, shaved, and brushed off one another to make sure they were meeting the expectation of the officers in charge. Now each were dressed neatly and stood erect in their formation. Their looks were exceeded only by their pride of being a pilot in the United States Air Force.

Soon every man's name was called. They each in turn walked before the officers, stopped, and snapped to attention with a quick salute. Afterwards the wings were pinned on each man, and they gathered back to form a line on the ground facing the platform.

The last man to receive his wings was Lieutenant Allen Livingston who was also honored as an outstanding student. This did not set well with Cunningham who thought Livingston had brown nosed those who taught them, but he kept his eyes forward as they were asked to accept the Airman's Creed.

The men stood proud as they repeated the Airman's Creed in unison:

I am an American Airman.
I am a warrior.
I have answered my nation's call.
I am an American Airman.
My mission is to fly, fight, and win.
I am faithful to a proud heritage,
A tradition of honor,
And a legacy of valor.
I am an American Airman.
Guardian of freedom and justice,
My nation's sword and shield,
Its sentry and avenger.
I defend my country with my life.
I am an American Airman.
Wingman, leader, warrior.
I will never leave an Airman behind,
I will never falter,
And I will not fail.

"I stood proudly on that day pledging to never falter or fail, but I had already faltered, and now I have failed miserably." Allen concluded his reminiscing and sat with his shoulders hunched.

Ling, always aware of Allen's needs decided to push Allen for further information. He knew that this release of emotions would begin a new healing that Allen desperately needed.

"How did you falter Allen?"

"Don't you see how I ran away from God? Just call me Jonah, because I ran away from the ministry, and the Lord let me be swallowed up in a burning F-105 and then spit me out in this remote land. He'll never use me now," lamented Allen.

"You forget, dear friend, that God did use Jonah, even after he had run. God may not use you as a minister, but He gave you talent and will surely give you a means to use it," offered Ling.

As Allen sat in contemplative silence, Ling pressed the second half of Allen's misery. "And why do you believe you have failed so many?"

"Ling, I should have been able to return to base with my squadron. Instead, I was shot down by enemy fire, and I obviously did something that made them deem me a traitor. I can only imagine what my parents and sister must be thinking and feeling. It makes me sick to think of the hurt they are suffering. Had I only stayed on the path the Lord had laid out for me, I'd be back in the States with my family and friends. Now I will never see them again."

"Why won't you ever see them again? You are almost healed completely. I am sure that Dr. Malin will be able to find a way for you to return to the United States."

"Ling, I have been called a traitor by my own country. How am I ever supposed to return? I couldn't put my parents through all of the humility," lamented Allen.

"But you are not a traitor, my friend. Surely your country will know that when you willingly return," offered Ling.

"No, Ling, they would have to have a trial. It would take a very long time for them to investigate where I have been and that I have made no contact with the enemy. All the while I would be kept in a prison."

"Surely your family knows that you would not do such a thing. I'm sure they would support you."

"Of course they would believe that I was completely innocent of the charges and support me through the whole trial, but I feel it would be better for them to believe that I am simply dead," finished Allen.

"But why would they think you dead?" questioned Ling.

"Because they know the only way I wouldn't be with my squadron is if I had died. They know that I would never have deserted my country. So it is better that they think me dead. At least that way they can mourn and go on with their lives. It won't matter that they will never see me again."

"I still do not understand why you feel you can never return," Ling pressed in confusion.

"How come, Ling, you have never returned to your home after all these years?" Allen suddenly asked.

"I could not subject my brothers to additional persecution," Ling quickly replied.

"I don't want to be persecuted either," echoed Allen.

It was clear to Ling by the tone of Allen's voice that their conversation was over. The sun had disappeared and all that was left were the deep purples coloring the horizon. It had been a long and emotional afternoon for the two friends.

Sorrow Left With Healing Music

Reminiscing the past and mixing those thoughts with his present situation caused Allen to fall into another state of depression. He barely spoke to Ling and asked Ping to quit coming altogether. Dr. Malin did all he medically knew how to do, but still Allen remained closed in his room.

Ling, determined not to let Allen's health fail again, insisted on taking him for daily walks.

He had confronted Allen after a week of his silence, "I will not let my friend die in his sadness. We will walk everyday. I will not talk until you decide it is time."

Allen looked at Ling and saw such trust in his friend's eyes. The sincerity with which Ling treated him touched his heart, but he was not ready to continue the story he knew Ling would ask to hear.

Days turned in to weeks as Ling continued walking daily with Allen. The silence continued between the two, but it wasn't uncomfortable. Ling spent the silence in prayer for his friend. He knew that talking would pull Allen out of his depression, but he wasn't sure how to get Allen talking freely again, so he remained supportive by his presence alone.

Ling remained completely silent as Allen sat with eyes closed pouring out his heart.

It appeared to Ling as if Allen was moaning when his next admission came forth. "I didn't pray about that decision. I simply chose to take my own self-made detour at that time. I wasn't going to follow the path God had laid out before me because it had gotten too confusing. I signed those recruiting papers and left my life in the charge of someone else for a while."

Now that Allen had begun speaking after such a long period of silence, his life's story couldn't seem to be stopped.

On a warm and partly sunny day, Ling left Allen's chair parked in the garden while he went to do an extra chore for Dr. Malin. As he and the doctor left the medical building they could see Allen staring at the clouds.

"Has he talked to you yet, Ling?" inquired the doctor.

"No, he has said not a word for over a month now."

"I believe today just may be the day he breaks his silence. Take as much time as you need this afternoon, Ling. I'll see to it that the afternoon chores are finished."

As Ling approached the garden he could see tears rolling down Allen's cheeks.

"Allen?" he quietly asked. "Do you want to talk today?"

"Ling," Allen sobbed, "I failed. I failed my God. I failed my country. I failed my family. "

Ling chose to remain silent and let Allen take as much time as he needed to gather his thoughts and feelings.

Allen found himself returning to the reality of where he was and what his future now held. Finishing his story with Ling had helped clear his conscious, and while he was still confused with the path the Lord had put him on, he was beginning to accept his fate and the peace and comfort being offered him by the Holy Spirit.

Allen's health also began improving greatly. His depression was lifting with each passing day, and he had begun putting weight on his leg. He found that he could get around rather well with the use of a cane. Dr. Malin kept a close eye on the healing of Allen's wound and encouraged him to begin walking more frequently for physical therapy.

It was on one of his outings that he decided to poke around in an old storage shed located in the back of the compound. While going through the rubbish he found a nice pile of lumber and several other items that caught his attention. A plan began to form in his mind as Allen instantly knew what he could do for the Lord in this remote location.

Hurrying back to the clinic he sought Ping's assistance.

"Ping, I know that you enjoy teaching the children, and with your musical education I'm wondering if you would be interested in helping me make some musical instruments for the children to learn to play."

Ping was surprised at the level of excitement that Allen was showing. She was so relieved to find him wanting to live that she simply stared at him for many seconds.

Allen, assuming her hesitation was negative, continued to persuade her, "I know that I pushed your friendship away recently, but I really believe that this could be a wonderful project for the compound's children and maybe even those who visit from neighboring villages. The music will be so enjoyable for them, and learning to play will give them something to make them proud. I can't do it by myself though. Please, Ping, say you will be willing to help me."

By the end of his speech Ping was smiling and began laughing as Allen's excitement took over. "Yes, I will help you, but how do we even begin? I know nothing of making musical instruments."

"My father was a master of making things from various materials, and he taught me well. After rummaging in the storage shed, I think we have most of the materials to begin making at least three or four instruments. I was planning on a couple guitars and violins. There will be a few things that we'll have to try and find, but I'm sure Dr. Malin and Ling could come up with the resources for those."

"Perhaps I will be able to help with those needed items also," offered Ping.

She said this with such conviction that Allen wondered, not for the first time, what Ping's personal story was. Other than her education, Allen had never learned where she lived or anything about her family; however, her quiet demeanor held an air of secrecy that made Allen hesitant about questioning her.

"We need to have Dr. Malin's approval before we begin," stated Allen.

Ping replied, "His wife, Dr. Angelika, loved music, and I'm sure that he will be very excited about your idea."

The two continued to discuss and make plans on how to carry out this mission as they went in search of Dr. Malin. After explaining their ideas to the doctor, he readily agreed that the children in the area would greatly benefit from such a program and offered his approval.

"You may use any of the materials in that old shed, and we have a supply of building tools and machines also. They aren't in the best of condition, but I believe most of them are still usable."

Allen and Ping finished making their plans and agreed to begin upon Ping's return the next morning. Allen found, with his excitement, that he wasn't able to sleep very well. The list of items he would need continued to grow in his mind, so he had gotten up early and was already going through the shed when Ping arrived.

"I've begun taking inventory and right now all we should need is varnish and some strings. I haven't found anything to make bows with either," Allen stated.

"Great," replied Ping. "Then where do we begin?"

Within the first couple of weeks Allen had constructed the basic shapes of the guitars and violins. Ping had managed to get the materials he needed and had begun recruiting young people who would be interested in learning how to play the instruments.

Allen worked long hours each day. Ping helped whenever she was available, and by the end of a month's time, they had their first four instruments tuned and ready.

The first day they were to have class, eight students excitedly showed up early at the compound to begin their music training. Among the eight were Li Snoog and his brother Ki. The brothers had been taking piano lessons already from Ping, but enjoyed music so much that they wanted to join the other children in class.

Allen and Ping were just as excited as the children. They had found a small room in the back of one of the compound's storage buildings that Dr. Malin allowed them to turn into a practice room. Now they sat facing their students with the compound's piano, their four homemade instruments, and six new instruments that had been donated by a friend of Ping's father laid out before them.

They took several days to evaluate the ability of each student and find where their musical interest lay. Then Allen and Ping began to prepare lessons for each student. The two shared the duties of teaching the basic rudiments and then Ping would work with the students whose acumen was more with string or wind instruments and Allen, who played piano by ear, would work with Li and Ki.

Li and Ki were more advanced in their basic knowledge, and after discussing the training process decided they wanted to continue with the piano as their main instrument of study. They were both quick to learn and developed their skills much faster than those just beginning. They naturally played by ear, so Allen, who had learned various techniques as a youth, was able to share much with them.

For months the two teachers spent hours each day training and teaching the students. They were extremely happy with the progress of their students. Some of which were beginning to play more than one instrument.

Since the classroom had been sectioned off for personalized training and practicing, the students were able to simultaneously learn their instruments and songs as they played their music scales. While the sound was often disconcerting, it was very pleasurable to Allen and Ping.

For almost half a year since Allen's initial idea came to life, the students worked diligently to learn their instruments. With much accomplished their first recital had been planned. Each student performed their chosen songs and played for their friends and family who joined them in the compound's garden.

Allen and Ping were extremely proud and couldn't wait to move into the next phase. The young people had shown so much natural talent and were learning at a rapid pace. So for the next six months Allen and Ping planned on working with the students to form a small orchestra.

Dr. Malin was so moved by the progress taking place in the compound. After the first recital he retreated to the family cemetery to talk with Angelika. "You would be so proud of Allen and Ping, Dear. They have done so much for the children here. They have made the children and their parents so proud. The music is bringing such happiness to our mission. You would have loved it. In fact, I'm sure that you would have been right in the middle of all of it. And Allen is making such great progress. Physically he has completely healed now, and I think his mental healing is almost under control too. I see him spending time in the Word again, and he has been teaching many songs of praise to the children. Your goal to provide healing is being achieved yet again. I wish you were here to share with me, but I can at least see you daily in this work I was privileged to begin with you. Until tomorrow, my Dear."

As Malin made his way back to the walled compound an idea came to him. He decided to send a letter to his friends and colleagues in Austria to seek donations of other instruments. He knew Angelika's church and friends would be happy to do this in her honor, since they were aware of her musical desire for these underprivileged children.

When the first shipment came from her church in Salzburg, Malin fell to his knees weeping at the sight of the gifts. He knew that the little orchestra he heard playing each day would be able to grow and progress knowing it was all due to Angelika. Even though she was gone, her influence still existed and he became more committed to seeing it continue.

A New Romance

After his heartbreak in college and with his Air Force training schedule Allen had almost stopped playing piano, but as he began teaching his new students he rediscovered his love for playing. He could often be found in the early mornings before class or on the weekends playing the old songs of his youth.

"You are playing a sad song today," Ping commented as she entered the classroom one morning. "Is something wrong?"

Allen and Ping had spent nearly every day together over the past year and they felt very comfortable in each other's presence. While she waited for his answer, she joined him on the piano bench and turned his song into a beautiful duet.

Allen had noticed more than just the ability of Ping's playing over the past year. He noticed the beauty of the young woman sitting beside him. He was impressed with her refined nature and found that she had claimed a special place in his heart. He knew it had begun when she was his attendant, but had truly grown when they joined to teach the boys and girls music.

The piano bench was small and they touched as they played. Allen found that he could not think clearly about playing. Placing his hands in his lap he stopped and watched Ping's graceful hands glide over the keys.

Allen's folks had taught him to be upstanding when he was a young man. Officer training taught him proper manners, and he knew what it was to be a gentleman and give respect to the opposite sex, but he found himself cautiously staring at Ping's profile. He couldn't get over how much he now loved her. He suddenly realized that he wanted to shout his feelings to the whole compound, but with Ping he found himself completely speechless and shy.

Allen was surprised when Ping solved this unexpected problem.

She suddenly did something she had not done up to this time. She stopped playing and looked directly into his face. Their eyes met and locked onto each other.

With just a single breath they both knew they were going to embrace. As Allen pulled her slowly, gently toward him, he was thrilled that she did not refuse. Their lips met each others with a light and warm caress. Her lips were as soft as a velvet cushion, and it was obvious to Allen that she had never kissed before. He reluctantly pulled away and said to her with a half apology, "I am sorry if I offended you, but I have wanted to do that for some time."

"It is not customary, in my family, to kiss, but I am glad that we have shared that together. I have felt for some time that I would like to be closer to you," admitted Ping.

"I am not able to stay any longer today," Ping told Allen as she took his hand and patted it.

"Thank you for this moment in my life," Allen told her as she gave him a beautiful smile before she turned to leave. Her silent promise to return made Allen's heart soar as he began to play a light-hearted melody. He cherished this young woman and looked forward to being with her the next morning.

However, Allen would have to wait an entire week before seeing Ping again. He had become concerned when she did not show up to the compound. He had questioned Dr. Malin about finding her, only to learn that Dr. Malin knew just as little about her as Allen did. The doctor knew that she was well educated and had more training than most of his volunteers, but he had never really questioned from where she came each day.

On the day that Ping did return she was very distraught and her normal smile was missing. "Ping, what is wrong?" questioned Allen.

"Allen, we need to talk." Ping led him to a set of chairs in the corner of the room. Allen could feel the dread swelling up inside his chest. He quietly sat after Ping had seated herself on the edge of the opposite chair.

"Allen, my full name is Princess Ping Savong. My father is the king of this country. I began coming to Friendship Mission because they were doing such great things for our people. I wanted to be able to work side by side with those who were offering such hope to those misplaced and underprivileged in my country."

Allen opened his mouth, but closed it again. He had no idea what to even say about this information he had just been given. Ping held up her hand to keep him from trying as she placed her fingers across his lips.

"Please, Allen, there is more. I have just found out this week that my family has arranged for me to marry an allied prince from our bordering country to the south. The wedding date has already been set. I will not be coming back after today."

Allen, completely stunned, began to stammer, "But, but do you even love this man?" He could see another love slipping out of his life, and he could feel the same heartache settling upon him.

"I don't even know this man," she quietly admitted.

"Then how can you marry him?" persisted Allen.

"It is not uncommon for marriages to be arranged for those in the monarchy. My parents do not understand your Christianity, and while I have enjoyed learning from you, I am from a Buddhist family," she explained. As her tears began to fall she tried further to help Allen understand. "I cannot bring dishonor to my parents."

Reaching for Allen's hands Ping poured her heart out with her next words. "Allen, I have learned to care for you very much . To love you even."

Allen could feel the sincerity of this beautiful young lady and his own tears began to form as she cried, "I know you will always be in my heart, but I must do the wishes of my parents." Allen knew how unselfish Ping was, and while he wanted to beg her to stay with him, he knew that he couldn't.

"You have a particular grace and calm that I adore. You have a level of sophistication that is so fitting with your beauty. I had a special feeling for you from the first time we met. I knew you were above all those around you. My heart cries out for you, your voice, the touch of your lips, and the touch of your finger tips just now. I don't know what I will do without your presence, but I understand your desire to not bring reproach on your family," Allen said in a subdued manner.

"I have already spoken to Dr. Rasmussen this morning. I told him who I am and asked him to find another he can train to do my chores." Ping took a brief moment to stare deeply into Allen's eyes. "You asked me once to do something for you, and I was slow to respond. I'm very glad that I had courage enough to pat your hand that first day. Now, I would ask that you do something for me."

Allen wasn't sure what she would want, but he had grown to trust and respect her like he had done only once before. "Sure, just ask," he answered.

"Would you kiss me just one more time and tell me you care?" she asked politely.

Allen stood, and still holding her hands, pulled her close to him. Lightly running his hands up her arms he embraced her. Laying his cheek against hers he whispered "I love you" in her ear. He knew this was the end of their relationship, and while he wanted this moment to last for a lifetime, he knew that he had to let her go.

He gazed into her tear filled eyes, then cupped her beautiful face in his hands and pressed his lips upon hers. His kiss was firm and held all the unspoken words between them. Slowly and reluctantly he pulled away. He could tell that Ping was not willing for the moment to end, but neither was he surprised when she removed his hands and walked away sobbing.

Allen could only stand and watch her retreating figure. As he allowed his tears to fall, he rubbed his hands together wishing she could have patted his hand before she left, but knowing that she was right.

He watched her from his door as she walked down the hospital hallway, stopping to hug Ling and then Dr. Rasmussen.

As she turned left at the front door of the big building Allen's tear drenched eyes followed her to a long limousine where she was met by a number of guards delegated to protect her. Soon the car disappeared as did the love of his last few years.

The relationship would not have been easy for them, and as Allen thought about the differences in their religions, he realized that a peace had already begun to settle another ache that had only moments ago threatened to occupy his heart.

Once again misfortune had come to Allen.

The Royal Wedding

Dr. Malin, Ling and his brothers were invited to Ping's wedding. Allen had also been invited, but he knew that it would be awkward for both him and Ping. He also couldn't set aside the fact that he was an American hiding out in a compound in a foreign land.

The day of the wedding was only a week away and would be held at the temple where the royal family had always attended with a number of monks officiating. Allen had learned some about Buddhists during his stay at Friendship Mission, but was still very unfamiliar with the beliefs of most in the area.

Ping had not discussed much about her and her family's faith during her visits with Allen. In fact, she seemed to have a sincere interest in Christianity, and unbeknownst to Allen she would compare the differences privately.

Allen was aware that Buddhism was the state religion and more than half of the country practiced it. One morning prior to the wedding Allen inquired of Ling to explain some of the beliefs held by Ping and her family.

Ling began by saying, "There are a number of different sections of Buddhism, and the beliefs of each group vary slightly. Most Buddhists believe in life as a process of change, moving towards greater wisdom, awareness and kindness. The mind is the decisive factor in the changing of the self, and meditation is used to develop the mind to a more positive state.

"The chief concern to Buddhists is that there is suffering in the world, but there is no sense of a creator God in Buddhism. The Buddha is a title and not a name, which means 'One who is awake to reality.' He was a human being who transformed himself, through enormous effort, to a state of profound Enlightenment."

"Do they have a teaching for them to follow or that instructs them?" Allen asked.

"Yes, they follow Dharma, the teachings of the Buddha where there is suffering, caused by wanting. This suffering can end completely by using the Eightfold Path which develops good understanding, thought, speech, action, work, effort, mindfulness, and meditation.

"Buddhism is an open religion that believes that all people are equal and it welcomes those of any age, gender, nationality or background," concluded Ling.

Allen wished he had known more about these beliefs so his conversations with Ping could have been more comparative. It seemed his beliefs were always bringing conflicts between him and those he loved. However, he was convinced what he believed was true and that the Bible, God's word to man, was the truth.

Ling, his brothers, and Dr. Malin had left to go to the palace the day before the wedding. They had been invited to stay in one of the guest rooms. This was a great honor, and Allen was excited for them, but he felt so alone with everyone gone from the compound.

He began thinking again of the information he had learned about Buddhism. One of the things that troubled him most was that it taught there were no supreme being, no sin, and no savior. According to Buddhist belief, the world keeps going through natural power, and there is no need for the existence of a personal creator. In fact, it denies the existence of a personal God.

Allen remembered from a conversation with Ping that Buddhism had even been called an atheistic religion because Buddha rejected all the gods of Hinduism which surrounded him.

Allen wished that he could have spent more time helping Ping understand more about his faith and Christianity. He wished he could have helped her see that people do sin against God and are in need of a savior.

As he sat thinking about Ping and her wedding to take place the next day, he remembered the words form Matthew 1:21: *"And she shall bring forth a son, and thou shalt call his name Jesus: for he shall save his people from their sins."*

Allen still cared greatly for Ping, but he knew that he couldn't develop a relationship with someone who did not share his Christian beliefs, and after Ling had shared so much more about Buddhism, Allen realized that she could never have married outside of her faith either and still remain in good grace with her family and country.

Three days later Allen's friends returned and Ling immediately sought his whereabouts. "How are you, my friend?" Ling questioned.

"I'm anxiously waiting for you to tell me all about the trip," replied Allen.

"The ceremony was a beautiful and festive affair. It was, of course, something like I have never experienced. It was very formal and filled with much activity foreign to us all."

Allen couldn't help but notice how excited and animated Ling's voice was. "So tell me all about the wedding ceremony," prompted Allen.

"It was much more than a typical Buddhist wedding, but with many similarities," Ling continued.

"It is traditional in some communities, on the morning of their wedding, for the bride and groom to visit a monk who has taken a vow of poverty and give him food in return for his blessing. Princess Ping and the Prince left very early that morning to keep with that tradition.

"Likewise, the bed has significance and an older couple may sometimes be called on to prepare the bridal bed and decorate it with lucky talisman such as bags of rice, sesame seeds, and coins. These symbolize fertility and happiness. Of course, I do not know if this is done by a Prince and Princess." Ling grinned and gave Allen a mischievous wink.

Allen rolled his eyes and groaned.

A Ceremony Allen Did Not Attend

"Come on, Ling! Quit teasing me and tell me about the wedding," Allen urged.

"Well, I brought you a program of the ceremony so you could read it yourself," Ling said handing it to him

Allen opened the folder and began reading:

King and Queen Sisavong Savong
Welcome you to share in the marriage of their daughter
Princess Ping Savong to Prince Souva Phuma

The service will begin with chanting:
Namo Tasssa Bhagavato Arahato Samma Sambuddhassa

Reply:
Homage to Him, the Exalted One, the Supremely Awakened One

Priest:
May the wisdom of the Blessed One shine within our
hearts, so that the mists of error and the foolish vanity of self
may be dispelled. So shall we understand the changing nature
of this life and strive to reach that spiritual peace which
the Buddha taught.

Friends, we have met together today in the presence of
this congregation, and in the sight of the Buddhas and
Bodhisattvas, to witness the vows of Prince Souva Phuma
and Princess Ping Savong.I earnestly ask anyone who
knows of any impediment to this marriage to make it known
now, or else remain silent."

The priest addresses the couple and says:
Before taking of these vows, remember that it is the duty of the husband to support and cherish his wife, to be faithful to her, to comfort her in sickness or sorrow, and to assist in bringing up the children. It is the duty of the wife to love and help her husband, to be patient and gentle in her manner, and to be faithful to him always.

The priest asks the woman: Will you take this man to be your lawful husband and remain faithful to him always?

Her reply: I will

The priest asks the man: Will you take this woman to be your lawful wife, and remain faithful to her always?

His reply: I will

The priest asks them both: Will you both undertake to sustain one another in sickness or in health, in happiness or in sorrow, and cherish one another at all times?

They reply: We will.

Priest: Duties of Husband described by the Buddha in the Sigalovada Sutta are:

1. *By honor*
2. *By respect*
3. *By faithfulness*
4. *By handing over authority to her*
5. *By giving her adornments*

In return for being cared for, a wife is compassionate to her husband:
1. *By doing her work well*
2. *By hospitality to her husband, relations and others*
3. *By faithfulness*
4. *By protecting what he earns*
5. *By skill and indulgence in all her duties*

The couple will chant the Three Refuges as they face the Buddha:

I take refuge in the Buddha
I take refuge in the Dharma
I take refuge in the Sangha

Priest to each in turn: I give you this ring, that you may place it on the finger of this woman/man, in token of your marriage to her or him, and may its circle remind you both of those things that are eternal.

The priest follows this by joining the couple's hands together by placing a string of beads rounds the wrists of their right hands and saying: Brother and sister, in the midst of worldly illusions with their fleeting glamour, try to preserve in your hearts truths taught by the Buddha. Be compassionate to all, and set your feet on the Path which leads from illusion and sorrow to Enlightenment and Peace. Since you have both agreed to marry according to Buddhist rite, I pronounce you to be husband and wife.

Priest: May the Blessed One receive you from this day forth as His faithful disciples, who take His teaching as your Guide. May peace be with you, and may wisdom and compassion surround you at all times.

Reply: Namo Amida Buddha (three times)

The marriage ceremony will conclude with chanting by the Community of Monks followed by meditation. The offering of lights will follow, and anyone who wishes to offer incense to the Couple is invited to do so.

"How did she look?" Allen inquired.

"Beautiful, with the look of a princess, sometimes with a slight smile and at times with sad looks," Ling had observed.

"The King and Queen, Ping's parents, were dressed majestically as I expected, but Ping was the center of attention. Her dress was outstandingly beautiful. It was accented with jewelry fitted to her personality and petite frame. Her head dress represented her role as a princess. It is so difficult for me to describe because I remember her at the compound without all the decorum. All I can say is she was gorgeous as she stood beside the Prince. I could tell she is well liked by her friends and the staffs of the palace appreciate her kindness," Ling added.

"Even though Ping and her husband are of a high royal caste, will they have to have certain items in their home or living quarters in the palace to be considered faithful Buddhists?" Allen asked.

"They will probably have a small home altar, a Buddha statue or other Buddhist deity statuary. They will have an incense burner with offering bowls and a small oil lamp. They will have religious paintings, or Thangkas, as they are called. They will have meditation cushions or benches along with copies of sacred text and sometimes the family will have a small meditation gong with a cushion and striker."

Allen and Ling began a long discussion on the differences between their Christianity and the Buddhist beliefs. They talked into the late evening hours till they had both grown weary. Ling left politely and Allen lay down on his bed, pulled his soft pillow under his head, and wondered about how happy Ping would be with the Prince. Saddened by his discussion with Ling, Allen unselfishly closed his eyes and offered a prayer for them both.

Becoming A Friend And Protector

Every evening after dinner Malin would rise from the table and walk to the door. It had become a ritual for him. He stopped to get his beret as he looked around to see if others were watching. The rest of the clinic knew of Dr. Malin's evening walk, and none would ever be found looking in his direction. They each knew that this was a private time for the doctor. Opening the door quietly, Malin proceeded down the same path he had taken for years.

Allen, who had decided to begin eating in the dining room, had watched Dr. Malin do this every day for several weeks. He, too, was totally aware of where the doctor was going. He thought about following, but decided to let Dr. Malin have his privacy.

The next evening the same routine began, except this time Dr. Malin motioned for Allen to join him. As they began to leave the compound gate, Allen said, "Thank you for inviting me to walk with you today. I know this is a very special and private time for you."

"You know where I go?" questioned Malin.

"Dr. Malin, everyone in the clinic knows what you do each evening. We all love you and respect your time. You do so much for each one of us that you deserve to have your evenings to yourself. Are you sure you want me with you?"

"Yes, I am a lonely old man with my angel gone. I enjoy our growing friendship," Malin answered.

This was the first time Allen had been very far from the clinic since he had been advised to stay in, but Dr. Malin explained that only a few ever came to this place which was hidden beyond those on the outside of the compound.

The pathway continued upwards and with every few yards the vistas seemed to change. Allen did not know there was such beautiful scenery surrounding the compound. His leg had healed, but this was the first long walk he had done with it, and he would welcome an opportunity to sit down.

Finally the two men arrived at a well kept private cemetery. Allen observed that there was one large headstone and four smaller ones beside it. Crudely chiseled on each stone was a name and date. Allen had only been at Friendship Mission for a short time when Dr. Angelika and daughter passed away, but he was curious about the other three stones. Given the dates, it was obvious that all three were infants. He knew, after having studied religions with Ling, that most every family in this area would have cremated their dead, so he questioned Dr. Malin about their identities.

"Those are my children," he quietly told Allen. "Angelika and I would have had a wonderful, large family, but the Lord chose to take them all from me."

As tears welled in Dr. Malin's eyes, Allen reverently walked to the edge of the cemetery. He was awed by the lush greenery and brilliant flowers surrounding him and became lost in the beauty. From this view he felt on top of the world and closer to the Lord than he had been in a long time. He was always amazed at God's creation and felt so humbled at what he was witnessing.

Almost reluctantly he turned to check on the doctor and found him kneeling beside Dr. Angelika's grave pulling weeds and talking. Allen felt that he had been invited along to support his friend, so he made his way back to the graves. He was soon within hearing distance, and his heart broke by the grief in Dr. Malin's voice.

"I am so lonely without you," he was confessing. "You know I would have never come to Laos if it wasn't for your concern for others. Sometimes I dream of returning home, but I will never leave you here alone," he promised.

As Dr. Malin sat pulling weeds, Allen approached him. "Dr. Malin," he hesitantly began, "Did you not want to do mission work here in Laos?"

"To be quite honest," Dr. Malin looked squarely at Allen, "I didn't want to do mission work anywhere. I would have been happy to follow my parents into the medical field and work in my local hospital or private practice. I fell in love with Angelika during medical school. She was so devoted to her Lord, and knew exactly what He had called her to do. I would have followed her anywhere."

"You didn't share the same devotion to God?" questioned Allen.

"I tried over the years to understand the Lord. Angelika told me from the very beginning that Christianity was about a relationship with God and not just about a religion. I do believe in God, but it was a growing thing with me. Angelika was the one with great faith and proved His presence time and time again here in this wilderness. I'm not sure I ever succeeded with my own relationship. I'm afraid I have let Angelika down. She talked so much of Heaven, and I know her and my children are there. I want to go where they are when I die, but I lack that confidence," he concluded.

Dr. Malin's statement immediately got Allen's attention. He knew Dr. Malin was a proud man, but also knew the way to heaven was the same for everyone.

"May I show you in the Bible how you can know for sure that you will spend eternity with your family?" asked Allen.

"Would you please," stated the doctor.

Allen removed the Bible he kept in his pocket. He opened to the New Testament book of Romans and read the ninth and tenth verses from chapter ten: *"If thou shalt confess with thy mouth the Lord Jesus, and shalt believe in thine heart that God hath raised him from the dead thou shalt be saved. For with the heart man believeth unto righteousness; and with the mouth confession is made unto salvation."*

"Angelika shared that verse with me several times, but never has it been so clear to me. I know what I must do now." Dr. Malin bowed his head and began to pray. He realized all his prayers before were said in a ritualistic manner, but this time it was coming from his heart. Tears were flowing freely down his cheeks as he lifted his head, turned to Angelika's stone, and said "I've made a real commitment now, my

Dear, and I know I will see you again."

That evening was the first of many trips Allen took with Dr. Malin to the cemetery. The walk was great exercise for Allen's mended leg, and it allowed his friendship with the doctor to continue growing. The two men were glad to share their dreams and hurts with each other.

On one evening trip Dr. Malin told Allen the whole story of Friendship Mission and how Angelika had been burdened with who would follow them. He shared his own concern for the people in that region who had been his family for so many years. "I am getting older, Allen, and since the Lord left me no heirs, I, too, often wonder who will follow us," he confessed. "Although the mission was not my original dream, I have grown to love these people, and I don't want them left without a place of refuge when I die."

"I am certainly thankful to have found refuge here," admitted Allen. As they slowly returned to the compound, Allen shared his love of music with Dr. Malin and thanked him once again for having given him the opportunity to use his talent in the compound. "Sharing music with the children has saved me from sure insanity," he laughed.

Upon entering the compound Dr. Malin motioned Allen to follow him to one of the warehouses. They stood in the doorway and waited for their eyes to adjust to the dimness found within. Dr. Malin made his way over to a covered object, and as he began removing the covering, he said "Angelika and I bought this piano in Vientiane at the beginning of last year."

Allen stood with his mouth wide open. "That's a Pleyel!" he exclaimed. "Do you realize what a prize you have?"

Dr. Malin smiled, "Yes, Angelika gave me the full history of this instrument. She had hoped to repair it so others could learn to play it. She always had a secret dream that one of the underprivileged of our area would become renown from being originally taught on that piano. Do you think you could restore it?"

Allen began dancing around the piano like a child on Christmas morning. As he touched the piano with awe he answered, "Yes, I know that I can. Oh, Dr. Malin, are you sure?"

"Yes, my boy. I am sure. I want you to restore this piano and use it for your own enjoyment as well as teaching the children."

After days of refurnishing the Pleyel, Allen had Ling and Lang help him move it to the small sitting area in the clinic. He felt that the children could continue learning on their older piano in the classroom, but could play their accomplished pieces in the clinic as a way of ministering to those who were ill and recovering.

Allen spent each morning playing the songs he remembered from years past. The beautiful sound of the piano was uplifting to everyone, and Allen found that God was once again mending his soul. He could often be found running his hands over the keys with his eyes closed in deep thought.

Malin, too, was having his soul mended. He would often stand out of sight and let the notes fill him with memories of Angelika and their life together. She had played those same beautiful songs each evening, and he knew that she would have been right in the middle of the music had she been there. A plan began to form in his mind, and after several days he approached Allen.

"Allen, you have a unique ability with your piano playing. I could spend hours listening to you. Have you ever thought of getting more training by a master teacher?" he asked with a serious voice.

"Yes, I wanted at one time to be as good as Beethoven, but that dream has died with many others," Allen answered.

A Beautiful Land Of Imprisonment

Allen and Dr. Malin eventually began walking together every evening. They shared their accomplishments and frustrations about their ministries. The compassion they had for those in the compound and surrounding villages continued to grow. Dr. Malin's desire for the success of the compound was multiplied when he fully gave his life to the Lord. Allen became more and more interested as he began to understand those he was working with.

"Dr. Malin, now that I have learned so much about the culture of the people in this area. I would like to know more about the area itself. Do you have any history that you could share with me?"

Dr. Malin chuckled as he answered, "My boy, you sound just like me many years ago. After I finally learned the ways of those people coming in and out of our compound, I decided that I needed to learn the history of the place I was now calling home. It's a rather colorful history, but I think I can easily piece it together for you.

"Did you know that this area was under the thumb of its neighbors at various times?" Dr. Malin began.

"Who were those neighbors?" Allen asked.

"They were the Cambodians, Burmese, Vietnamese, Chinese, and Siamese. And because of them this area had great difficulty in establishing a national identity. The earliest inhabitants of this area were migrants from southern China, but with time other groups began to come into this region.

"In fact, when Souligna Vongsa died in 1694 without an heir, the leadership of Lan Xang was contested, and the nation split into three kingdoms. The area around Vientiane was taken over by Souligna's nephew, supported by the Annamites from northern Vietnam. Souligna's grandson controlled the area around Luang Prabang while another prince with Thai backing controlled the area of the southern kingdom of Champassak. China, Burma, and Vietnam briefly held sway over these kingdoms; bands of Chinese marauders terrorized the north of the country. So you see, Allen, that is why this area continues to this day to be without a leadership with full control. Centuries of conflict have existed incited by groups wanting to enlarge their borders. Am I boring you?"

"No! I am finally learning the circumstances surrounding my friends and me. Is there more you can share?"

"Oh, yes. In the late 19   "So that is why this whole area was called Indochina," Allen stated.

"Yes, but the French didn't think too highly of the protectorate," Dr. Malin announced. He continued with more reasons for the condition around the Rasmussen's Friendship Mission. "The French saw the land was too mountainous for plantations, there was little in the way of mining, and the Mekong River was not suitable for large commercial navigation.

"The French built very few roads. The main route was the Colonial Road constructed to connect the cities from Luang Prabang through Vientiane to Savannakhet and the Cambodian frontier. We traveled much of that road to get here and by modern day standards it isn't much of a road," Dr. Malin explained.

"This area has had little opportunity to better itself. You see, the French built no higher education facilities and made only a half-hearted attempt to cultivate rubber and coffee. The main export under the French was opium," lamented Dr. Malin.

"Only a few hundred French resided in this area, and they adopted an immoral lifestyle and left the running of the place to Vietnamese civil servants. There has been little change in the people of this area as they carried on farming as they had for hundreds of years. During the Colonial period administration, health care, and education made hardly any impact or progress.

"The 50-year French sojourn here came to an abrupt end in March 1945 when the Japanese took control of the government of this area. The French granted full sovereignty to the area in 1953, but the Pathet Lao regarded the royalist government as Western dominated. When in 1954 the French made a last stand at Dien Bien Phu, it ended badly, with a stunning defeat.

"The weary French started a withdrawal from Indochina. At this point, the United States started supplying the Royal Lao Government with arms. That government ruled over a divided country from 1951 to 1954.

"Prince Souvanna Phouma, a neutralist, operated from Vientiane in the south. Right-wing, pro-United States Prince Boun Oum of Champassak dominated the Pakse area. In the far north, Prince Souphanouvong led the leftist resistance movement, the Pathet Lao, drawing support from North Vietnam.

"Souvanna Phouma became Prime Minister in 1956 and tried to integrate his half-brother's Pathet Lao forces into a coalition government. That government was toppled just a couple of years before you crashed near our compound. Once again war is brewing between the Royal Lao Army and the Pathet. It wouldn't surprise me if it happens in the near future," Dr. Malin concluded.

"Wow, you know your history! Did you feel safe to operate your clinic all this time?" questioned Allen.

Dr. Malin, who knew he was no hero, admitted, "There were several occasions that I wanted to get Angelika out of here, but she was always quick to remind me that we had a special hand of protection over us."

The doctor was fully aware that for decades the area around the compound had been plagued by civil war, coups, countercoups, and chaos. His knowledge revealed that the area had become a pawn of the superpowers, with Hmong tribesmen trained by CIA agents, Thai mercenaries fighting for the Royal Lao Government, and the Pathet Lao receiving help from the Chinese, the Russians, and the Vietminh.

"I couldn't keep up with the number of coups and even heard it confused the Americans who were unsure of which Phoumi, Phouma, Phoui, Souvanna, or Souvanou was in power at any given time," he chuckled.

"For more than thirty years I have lived in an area filled with guerillas, communist agents, Special Forces troopers, armed tribesmen, opium growers, an international corps of mercenaries and sundry camp followers. This area was thrust on the world stage with the Vietnam war and has thus suffered through heavy bombing with the subsequent loss of people and governmental infrastructure. It is one of the poorest countries on the planet as most of its citizens are lacking in education and useful training. While Angelika and I could have lived our lives as wealthy doctors, we chose to follow the calling the Lord gave to Angelika. Because of that calling we have been able to make a difference in the lives of many displaced peoples here in south Asia. Stick around long enough and you will find that you love the people as much as I have come to love them," finished the doctor.

The Helper Is Found

Over the years, the Rasmussens had helped many people in South Asia. They trained many to plant crops and barter for their needs and others were taught building trades. With the lack of educational facilities, the Rasmussens also found it important to teach the area peoples how to read and write. There were many who became very skilled and went back to their own villages to teach their families and friends. The Rasmussens were fortunate that those who were seeking refuge or had lost their home would stay and help them teach others.

After Dr. Angelika passed away, Dr. Malin knew that he would not likely find a doctor to replace her, but he was in need of someone who could share her duties. He began praying in the same manner he knew Angelika would have, asking God to provide the exact person to fill his need.

Song Soo's parents had been killed in the governmental unrest, and she had fled her North Vietnam home looking for assistance from the great oppression. After getting into Laos she began to hear about a compound that helped people and finally found her way there. Dr. Malin gladly welcomed her into the compound.

"We will be happy to do whatever we can to help you, Song Soo. We are a working compound, though. Have you been trained for any certain skill?" he questioned.

"I am a trained nurse, Dr. Malin. I worked in a small clinic in my home town. I'm sure that I could be of assistance to you, and I am not scared of hard work," she quickly answered. She knew she had nowhere else to turn and hoped that she might find her refuge in their compound.

Song Soo was surprised by the doctor's response. With tears in his eyes he looked heavenward and whispered, "Thank you. You did it again." Then looking at her he said, "I will have Lang show you to a room and let you get rested from your journey. I would like for you to join me in the clinic tomorrow morning."

"Yes, sir, I will be there at sunrise." Song Soo was thrilled to have found such good fortune. She immediately began showing how beneficial she would be in the clinic, and while she was a Hindu, she did not find it hard working with the Christians or the majority of Buddhists in the compound.

Lang Kai, while younger, befriended the young lady on every possible occasion. While he was a Christian from China, there were many teachings that were similar to them.

Lang knew Hindus, contrary to popular understanding recognized one God, Brahman, the eternal origin who is the cause and foundation of all existence. However, he could never understand the reason for so many gods under him.

One day while eating lunch together, Lang asked Song Soo to answer that question. Song Soo said, "There are many gods of the Hindu faith representing different expressions of Brahman. Hindus recognize three principal gods: Brahma, who creates the universe; Vishnu, who preserves the universe; and Shiva, who destroys the universe."

Lang was listening intently as she continued, "Brahma is the creator. However, Brahma is not worshipped in the same way as other gods because it is believed that his work, creation, has been done."

Lang, having trouble understanding Song Soo's views, asked her if his brother could meet with them to help explain the differences in Christianity and Hinduism. Song Soo readily agreed and they planned to meet the next afternoon.

Gathered for tea in the clinic's small lounge, Ling and Song Soo had the opportunity to get better acquainted. Even though Song Soo had been working in the clinic for quite some time her and Ling's assignments hadn't allowed them to form a friendship. Ling told Song Soo of his family's religious history.

"My grandfather and father had been Buddhists before Father decided that Christianity offered more solutions and met his spiritual needs better." "I'm afraid that I don't know all the history of Buddhism," admitted Song Soo.

"Let me start from the beginning then," Ling offered. "Siddhartha Gautama founded Buddhism about 500 years B.C. He was the son of a king in southern Nepal who was warned by a sage that his son would become an ascetic. Because of this he was never allowed to leave the palace. However, he escaped and became a beggar spending his time searching for peace.

"It is said that Gautama fell into deep meditation under a fig tree called the Bodhi – the tree of wisdom. There he reached the highest degree of God-consciousness known as Nirvana. He spent 40 years teaching the truths he learned. Thus, he became known as the Buddha or Enlightened One.

"His understanding of the origin of suffering constituted the basis of Buddhism. First, he taught that everyone must suffer. Second, the cause of suffering came by selfish craving. Thirdly, Buddha taught craving can be overcome and after defeating it you can enter the state of Nirvana and all suffering ends. The way to end craving is the Eightfold Path."

"I have heard of the Eightfold Path," interjected Song Soo.

"Well that is the basic to Buddhism. My father once had an interest in Hinduism since Buddhism had its origin in it, but he knew that the Veda taught there were 33 main deities that were meant to bring peace and to ward off evil spirits. He began to question the pantheistic views and was not satisfied with the Hindu explanation that there is one god, but has 33 facets.

"He also didn't understand the need for numerous Hindu scriptures; namely, the Vedas, the Great Epics, which consists of the Ramayana and the Mahabharata that includes the Bhagavad-Gita," Ling concluded. "Do you practice all this in your beliefs, Song Soo?" he asked.

"Well, not all," was her reply. "I was taught that the supreme god lives in all creatures, both humans and animals. Because of it we believe all life is sacred. I was taught the cow was the most sacred since it gives so much."

Song Soo opened a book she had with her. "Read with me in the Atharva Veda," she said. *"'Worship to thee springing to life, and worship unto thee when born! Worship, O Cow, to thy tail-hair, and to thy hooves, and to thy form!' A little further it says, 'The Cow is Heaven, the Cow is Earth, the Cow is Vishnu, Lord of Life. He who hath given a Cow unto the Brahmans winneth all the worlds. Both Gods and mortal men depend for life and being upon the Cow. She hath become this universe: all that the Sun surveys is she.'*

"I believe a social hierarchy existed," continued Song Soo. "The Brahmans who were the elite linked with the priesthood. The Kshatriyas are the Military and ruling class. The Vaisyas were made up of the farmers and businessmen, and finally, the Sudra were the peasants."

"Hmmm! That is interesting and one of the reasons my father left his faith for Christianity. We discussed this very thing, and he pointed out a verse in the Bible. I'd like for you to read it with me." Ling got out his Bible and turned to Galatians 3:28. *"There is neither Jew nor Greek, there is neither slave nor free, there is neither male nor female; for you are all one in Christ Jesus."*

Lang, who had been sitting quietly through their conversation, said, "Now that you have shared such history, I am finally putting all the pieces together."

Ling And Song Soo's Dialogue Continues

The next day Ling was hoping to visit with Song Soo again. After getting to finally know her, he found that he couldn't resist being with her. Her personality and demeanor were very enticing to him. He inwardly rejoiced when Lang told him that Song Soo wanted to finish their conversation of the day before.

Song Soo, Ling, and Lang had openly discussed their differences in a spirit of love. They were willing to accept each other's convictions with understanding and without judgment. As they got comfortable in the lounge once again, it was apparent that they were all three eager to begin another discussion.

Ling chose to bring up the subject of salvation. "Song Soo, what do the Hindu's say is the way to salvation?"

She answered by saying, "It is achieved in one of three ways: first, through knowledge; second, through devotion by obeying a particular deity; or thirdly, through good deeds."

"That's interesting," Lang replied. "As Christians we believe that you can't earn your salvation through doing any specific thing, but that we are saved by Jesus."

"That's right," Ling began as he flipped through his Bible. "We believe that redemption of our sins comes through Jesus. Let me read Romans 3: 23 and 24, *'For all have sinned and come short of the glory of God, being justified freely by His grace through the redemption that is in Christ Jesus.'*"

"I do not understand how Jesus can save a person from the sins that they have committed. Jesus did not commit those sins," Song Soo commented.

"That is correct. Everyone has sinned and must pay for those sins. Each person should be punished with eternal separation from our sinless Father, God. God, however, loves His people so much that he does not want to be separated from them, so He allowed His son, Jesus, to take the punishment for everyone's sins in order that those who believe in Jesus will live eternally with Him and the Father, God," Ling explained.

"So your God loves you and will help you if He can?" she questioned.

"Yes, He helps us every minute of our day. We need only ask Him," Lang quickly answered.

"Hmm," she quietly said. Ling and Lang could tell that she was in deep thought. It was several minutes before she continued. "As a Hindu we were taught to pray to images to find help in worship. In the Bhagavad-Gita 12 it says, *'The Supreme Personality of Godhead said: Those who fix their minds on My personal form and are always engaged in worshipping Me with great and transcendental faith are considered by Me to be most perfect,'*" Song Soo pointed out.

"Not to offend you, Song Soo, but your images are not alive. Our God is alive. He is the creator of all that you can see. He tells us in the Bible, Exodus 20: 3-6, *'You shall have no other gods before Me. You shall not make for yourself a carved image - any likeness of anything that is in heaven above, or that is in the earth beneath, or that is in the water under the earth; you shall not bow down to them nor serve them. For I, the Lord your God, am a jealous God, visiting the iniquity of the fathers upon the children to the third and fourth generations of those who hate me, but showing mercy to thousands, to those who love Me and keep My commandments.'* If we love God, our creator, with pure devotion, then He will love us unconditionally in return. We don't ever have to worry about not being good enough for God if we keep His commandments and accept His son's redemption for our sins," Ling added.

"Then let me ask you this," Song Soo slowly began. "If your god will love you unconditionally and not expect you to work for your salvation, then what about reincarnation. How do you ever get the chance to better yourself?"

"Reincarnation is something that I don't fully understand," answered Lang.

Ling shook his head in agreement. "Will you tell us more about your belief in it?"

"I was taught that if a person lived a virtuous life he could reach a high state through rebirths. It is 're-entering the flesh.' When you die you come back as another person or as another animal. One can reach a stage called 'mutki' when reincarnations cease," Song Soo replied.

"Our Bible does not teach or support what you have said of reincarnation. It says in Hebrews 9:27, *'And as it is appointed for men to die once, but after this the judgment.'* Christians believe that we have one death and after that death we will be with our Lord in Heaven. There is nothing better than being in that place," Ling assuredly told her.

"There are so many things that are different between your Christianity and Hinduism. What else can you tell me, Ling?" questioned Song Soo.

"I learned quite a bit more from my father, but I don't want to bore you," said Ling.

"Please," says Song Soo. "I would like to know. This is very interesting to me."

"One of the most important differences is that Hinduism is pantheistic, not theistic. God created the world out of nothing rather than out of His own substance. That simply never occurred to anyone but the Jews and those who learned it from them. Everyone else either thought of the gods as part of the world, which would be paganism, or the world as part of God, which is pantheism.

"Furthermore, if God is in everything, God is both good and evil. If that is the case, there is no absolute morality, no divine law, no divine will discriminating good and evil. You see, in Hinduism, morality is practical; its end is to purify the soul from desires so that it can attain mystical consciousness. Only the God of the Bible is absolutely righteous.

"Next, Hinduism comes from a private mystical experience; while Christianity is recorded in a book called the Bible which is a summarized creed.

"In Hinduism there are many levels of truth: polytheism, for one, with the belief of sacred cows and reincarnation for the masses; monotheism, for the mystics, who declare the individual soul one with Brahman, making truth relative to the level of experience.

"Christianity tells you to love your neighbors; Hinduism tells you that you are your neighbors.

"Song Soo, there are two essential points of Christianity – sin and salvation – and both are missing in Hinduism. If there is no sin, no salvation is needed, only enlightenment. We need not be born again; rather, we must merely wake up to our innate divinity. If I am part of God, I can never really be alienated from God by sin.

"I don't want you to think I am preaching or being aggressive with my beliefs, but I came from what you were taught to believe, to a new, and what I feel, is a better life, validated by Holy Scriptures of a living savior."

"Oh, no! I am finding what you are telling me very interesting and something of which I am totally unaware," Song Soo replied. "Is there more I should know?"

"There is more that I would like to share. After our conversation yesterday I began thinking about my own beliefs and why Christianity is so important to me. I wrote several things down, and I would love to read them with you and Lang. I think it is important for him and me to both keep our beliefs fresh in our minds.

Ling suggested she take her pad and pencil and write the things he was going to share with her.

"I'm ready!"

Then Ling began with a list of his beliefs.

"First, Christians believe that the Bible is the uniquely inspired and fully trustworthy Word of God. It is the final authority for Christians in matters of belief and practice, and though it was written long ago, it continues to speak to believers today.

"Second, Christians believe in one God in three persons. He is distinct from His creation, but intimately involved with it as its sustainer and redeemer.

"Third, Christians believe that the world was created once by the divine will, was corrupted by sin, yet under God's providence moves toward final perfection.

"Fourth, Christians believe that, through God's grace and favor, lost sinners are rescued from evil thoughts, words and deeds.

"Fifth, Christians believe that it is appointed for human beings to die once and after that face judgment. Those who respond to His grace will have eternal life. Those persisting in rebellion will be lost eternally.

"Sixth, Christians believe that spirit beings inhabit the universe, some good and some evil, but worship is due to God alone.

"Seventh, Christians believe that God has given us a clear revelation of Himself in Jesus and the sacred Scriptures. He has empowered ministers to guide us into faith and holiness in accordance with His Word.

"Eighth, Christians believe that Jesus is God incarnate and, therefore, the only sure path to salvation. Many religions may offer ethical and spiritual insights, but only Jesus is the Way, the Truth and the Life.

"We are taught in our Bible in the book of Acts chapter 4 verse 12: *'Nor is there salvation in any other, for there is no other name under heaven given among men by which we must be saved.'*"

Ling finished his list of beliefs with this thought for Song Soo,

"There are many similarities, but far more differences. I believe we only need one God who is the creator of all things. Hindu and Buddhist beliefs lay more in one's self for his future. We are taught there is none good and our salvation comes from Jesus Christ who was our sacrifice."

"You have given me many things to think about and offered me solutions I had never heard of before. Thank you for taking the time to explain your Christianity to me and for being so understanding of my beliefs at the same time," replied Song Soo. "And, Lang, thank you for inviting your brother and for joining our conversation again today. It appears I have a lot to consider. You both know your beliefs much better than I know my own."

As Ling departed he prayed that he had not broken what he hoped would become a growing relationship between Song Soo and himself. They had both lost their families in a similar way and had escaped imminent death before finding Friendship Mission. He wanted to get closer to her and spend their free time together.

From that day on, Ling, Lang, and Song Soo became close associates working side by side. Because of her nurses training she began making rounds with Ling and Dr. Malin. After having learned so much about Christianity she began to observe how their lives were different from her own, and she knew it was because of the failures in her own religious life.

A Hard The Way Out

Allen was surprised when Dr. Malin burst in on his music lessons one morning. Dr. Malin wore a broad grin and all but yelled, "Pack your bags, my boy, you're headed for Austria." He grabbed Allen's hand and while shaking it embraced him in a tight hug.

Allen, completely shocked by the news, could only stand and stare at his friend. When the doctor offered no more information, and actually appeared ready to leave the room, he managed to say, "What are you talking about? I'm not planning on going anywhere."

"Yes, you are, and you are leaving in three days. I have already made plans for you to study under my good friend Karl at the University of Vienna. He was my roommate in college and is very successful. We have stayed in touch all these years. He is a faithful supporter of Friendship Mission. In fact, he still sends me my portion of rent from the apartment we shared." Waving his hand in the air he continued, "Oh, I'm too excited to keep my thoughts together. Karl still has the apartment and you will stay with him. He will teach you to be an accomplished pianist."

"But, Dr. Malin," began Allen.

"No buts, my boy. I just received your passports and papers of citizenship from Princess Ping. She was more than willing to help. Ling is finalizing the rest of your trip today. It appears as if everything will be a go in three days."

"Wait." Allen put his hands up to stop the doctor and motioned him to move out of his students' hearing range. "First, I can't leave the compound with the military searching for me, and second, is Ling leaving too?"

"Yes, Ling and his brothers are returning to China. They have wanted to go home for several years. Now that the wars are somewhat calm, it is the perfect time for all of you to leave and travel together."

"The wars around here may be calming, but you can bet the United States is still looking to hang me," Allen countered. "I'm not going to face that Dr. Malin, and I'm not going to live my life looking over my shoulder all the time. I'm happy right here, and here is where I will stay."

"Allen Livingston can stay here if he wants, because," said the doctor pulling papers out of an envelope and handing them to Allen, "Paul Allen Rasmussen will be the one leaving." He showed Allen the passport and citizenship papers that Princess Ping had processed for him.

"I thought it would be okay with you if I shared my name. You have been like a son to me over the past few years. It is time for you to get out of here, and while I'm still not sure I agree with you not going back to your country and taking care of that traitor business, I am still intent on helping you with this area of your life. You may continue to be called Allen since that is your middle name. Ping thought of that. She has been a great asset. She has gotten the Kai brothers all the paperwork they will need also."

"But who will teach my students?" Allen countered. "And who will help take care of you?"

"Allen, do you want to go?" Dr. Malin became serious as he asked this question. "Do you want to fulfill this dream of yours?"

"More than anything, but it's so sudden. I'm scared," Allen admitted. "I guess I sound ungrateful with those excuses and all. I am very thankful, and if you believe it can work, then yes, I want to go."

"I have prayed for many months, my boy. God has put every detail into place. Li and Ki Snoog will be taking over the instructions with your students, and Song Soo will take good care of me. I will miss our nightly walks together, but I know this is the right thing for you to do."

Allen turned and walked slightly away, "Well, my students, it looks like I'll be saying goodbye."

The next three days flew by in a whirlwind. Allen quickly caught the excitement of his two dearest friends, Dr. Malin and Ling. They went over the route Ling proposed and it appeared to be sound. Allen spent his final two nights walking with Dr. Malin and Ling spent his with Song Soo.

The morning of the departure was beautiful. The sun was bright and the sky very blue. Everyone in the compound had gathered to send the four young men on their way. There were many handshakes and hugs along with laughter and tears. Allen was taken aback when he saw Ping come walking through the crowd.

"I needed to come and say goodbye to my friends," she said as she looked from one to the other. "You are all so very special to me, and I am sad for you to go, but so happy for you to have your dreams coming true." Although she wore a brave smile, Ping had tears in her eyes as she hugged each one in turn.

When she got to Allen she said, "You gave me so much. I hope that you will find your happiness."

"Thank you for all that you have done to make this possible for me. You know that I will always cherish our time together," Allen said while looking into her eyes.

The crowd had begun pressing in again and all Allen could do was mouth a quick goodbye to Ping. He noticed Song Soo was tearfully telling Ling goodbye. He knew the two had been spending a lot of time together, but before he could think further about that relationship he found himself engulfed by Dr. Malin. The two held each other in a tight embrace, and it was then that Allen felt his own tears begin to fall.

"You saved me physically, and now you are really giving me back my life," Allen sobbed.

While Allen struggled with his emotions Ling addressed Dr. Malin, "You gave my brothers and me a place to take refuge. We owe you for our lives."

"Now you are giving us all a new beginning," Allen said. "You are the most generous person I know. You have given your life for so many others here. I wish I knew how to thank you."

"There is no thank you needed, my boy. All four of you just promise to do your best wherever you are."

All four young men gave their promise and Allen added, "If the Lord is willing, we will plan to see you here again, but if not here, we'll see you in Heaven."

After one more tight embrace, Allen and the Kai brothers started the first leg of their trip. They would walk twenty miles west of the compound to the Mekong River. Ling had made a deal with a riverboat captain for them to work for their passage.

Allen had no idea that the Mekong was one of the world's major rivers. He later learned from the captain that it is the tenth longest river in the world and roughly 3,000 miles from beginning to end. He was relieved when he learned they would only be traveling half that distance.

The boat trip would last two weeks. Allen and the Kai brothers were expected to help with the loading and unloading of the cargo. The trip was long and hard, but the four friends were sure to get a daily lesson about the river. They enjoyed listening to the rugged ship captain who had made the trip a number of times and would always find interesting information to share.

"The Mekong River begins, like the Yangtze, the Bramaputra and the Salween, 16,400 feet on the Tibetan Plateau. It tumbles to the Mekong Delta and the South China Sea.

"It flows through the rainforests of Xishuangbanna, skirts Myanmar and plays politics as the border between Thailand and Laos. It is there that it becomes the lifeline of a country.

"Heading south, the Mekong enters Cambodia and instead of flooding during periods of high waters, it backs up into a channel called Tonle Sap, 'Great river or lake,' where it fills a lake and irrigates one of the world's most fertile rice bowls. This natural wonder helped feed the great Khymer Empire called Angkor.

"The Mekong makes a magic change at the border with Vietnam. It divides into dozens of tributaries and becomes the Cuu Long or Nine Dragons. This vast, fertile rice growing region that is the Mekong Delta is where the great river mixes with the tropical waters of the South China Sea.

"The story of the Mekong region is written by the tapestry of people who have made it their home. The area has served as a land bridge between Asia, Australasia and even the West. First there were the Melanesians who later moved south to islands such as New Guinea.

"A migration of Mongoloids from China and Tibet began hundreds of years before Christ and became the ancestors of present day Malays, Dais, Bais, Khymers, Mons, Burmans, Viets, Hmongs, Kadais, Laos, Miaos, Mons, Tais, Akhas, Yeos and other tribes that moved south through the river valleys as Chinese power consolidated.

"It was the Indian traders in search of gold and spices during the first century who brought their Hindu-Buddhist culture to the region." The captain, Allen was sure, could have continued with his information for many more days, but the last four days they had been on the river was inundated with rain and they all chose to keep as dry as possible rather than gather together and talk.

The boat finally docked at a port in the province of Yunnan in the far southwestern corner of China. The Kais were from Bai, one of twenty-five ethnic minorities in the Yunnan Province. Ling had told Allen of the area's beautiful landscape. "It ranges from snowy mountains to tropical rainforests. There are clear, pure lakes, forests of stone and the ethnic minorities honor their traditions every day." Allen couldn't help but notice how Ling had such a homesick look in his eyes as he talked about his land. Allen was glad for him to be returning home even though he knew the reunion would be bittersweet.

Each one thanked the captain for his transportation before they headed out on foot once again. Ling had explained that they would need to follow the old Burma Road to reach Kunming, the capital of the Yunnan Province. Kunming was the home of Ling's birth and where he hoped to find many old friends after nearly eleven years being gone. The trip, most of which would wind them through rugged mountains, would take over two weeks if they had to walk the entire distance. Ling hoped they would find someone who was willing to transport them, but they had little money and knew they should conserve it for future emergencies.

The Lord was faithful to the four tired men as they traveled. They were able to find enough vegetation along the way to sustain their hunger and camping out through the nights in the lush forests was not a problem for them. They had so few possessions when they left Laos that each had only a small bag slung over his shoulder. On several occasions the Lord provided someone with a truck who allowed the four to climb on the back and ride.

As they got closer to the city, the Kai brothers became more excited and seemed to walk quicker with each passing mile. Ling and Lang told many stories of their past life in Kunming and Noi, who had been so young when they fled, was getting anxious to see all the places his brothers were describing.

After only ten days, the young men were entering the city. As they entered, Ling began remembering the location of his uncle's home. In a short time they arrived and amid the shouts of surprise they were greeted with warmth and hugs.

Ling had not changed much, as his kindred pointed out, but Lang and Noi had been so young when they left that their years of maturing had occurred while they were away.

Ling's cousins asked many questions about where they had been living since leaving China. Ling began to cry as he began to share the mercy and love of the Rasmussens as they took in the three.

"They gave us a place to live, food to eat, and trained us to help others," Lang added for his brother.

"And we made friends we could trust," added Noi.

"I would like to ask if Lang and Noi can live here with you, my Uncle," Ling questioned.

"I will not be a strain on your family, because I am now trained as a medical technician and can contribute to the family needs," Lang promised.

"And I will learn a trade too," Noi stated.

"But what will you do?" his uncle questioned.

"I am going to accompany Allen into Austria," he answered.

"What?" questioned Allen. "You are finally home. Why would you continue on with me?"

"I have more knowledge about traveling through Asia. You will need me to help get you there safely," Ling stated.

After further discussion among the family, the plans for Lang and Noi were set. Now Ling had to finalize the second leg of his and Allen's trip. He planned to see if they could hitch a flight on a plane that was owned by a close friend who flew cargo to various cities.

While they were waiting, Ling's uncle told Allen about Kim Hoo, a pilot friend. "Kim has been a friend of ours for many years. He was a member of the house church we grew up in and is still a practicing Christian."

Ling suddenly burst through the door bubbling with excitement. "We are blessed! Kim Hoo is flying cargo to Alamaty, Kazakhstan; and afterwards on to Moscow, Russia. It will be in a few days, but he says we can go. It is going to be a long flight. We will have many stops for rest, sleep and refueling, but we will be on our way."

God Has Provided

Ling enjoyed having a few days to see his homeland and share stories with his family. He was thankful that he could see his brothers get settled in their uncle's house before leaving them. The three brothers spent many hours together talking about the life they had shared since their parents were killed. They relived the sorrows and rejoiced again for the blessings. Lang and Noi both agreed that Ling needed to continue on the trip with Allen. They knew how much Ling loved Allen and looked to him as an older brother. They were glad for Ling to have such a friendship in his life of hardships.

On their fourth morning in Kunming, the brothers and Allen awoke early to prepare for another round of goodbyes. The whole family gathered together in prayer and asked the Lord for His protection as Ling and Allen traveled and for a peace to bridge the distance between the brothers.

As Ling embraced his two younger brothers he felt overwhelmed with emotion. He knew that he was doing the right thing by continuing with Allen, but he had been his brother's protectors for so many years that he felt he was abandoning them. "I will stay if you ask me to," he told them.

Lang answered for both brothers, "You have done your part to raise us, Ling. You were both father and mother when we needed you. It is time for you to live your own life. We will be well kept here with Uncle, and you know that the Lord is the greatest keeper either of us could have."

"Thank you, my brother. You are right." Looking at both Lang and Noi he continued, "I will leave you in His hands. I will return to you as soon as He is willing. Until then, I will write to you as often as I can. May His blessings be abundant for you."

Before the sun had cleared the mountains, Ling and Allen

boarded Kim's cargo plane and prepared to leave Kunming. The plane was full of items to be delivered at various cities between there and Moscow. The plane engines roared and it took off into rough winds. Once they cleared the mountains the turbulence eased and they settled in for the first leg of their flight.

Once in Moscow, Ling and Allen helped Kim with the unloading process. Three hours later the plane was empty, they paid Kim for his transport, and stood wondering about their next move.

"If you take that hall off the terminal there, you will enter the passenger services area. You can find out when the next flight heads west," offered Kim. "After I finish my paperwork, I'll come make sure you have things settled before I take off again."

"Thank you," both Ling and Allen said as they started for the hall.

Being an American in a foreign land was not as acceptable as being Oriental, so Allen stood back as Ling discussed flights with various attendants.

"We have a flight in the late afternoon to Vienna, Austria. There is a short layover at Budapest, Hungary. Would you like tickets for two?" she asked.

"Please," answered Ling as he handed her his and Allen's passports.

The attendant, looking at the two men, glanced at their passports and noticed they were from Laos. She thought Allen may have been French since Laos was once a protectorate of France. It had been wise for Allen to remain silent as his speech would have betrayed his nationality.

Combining all the money they had, Ling paid for their tickets and turned away with a look of concern on his face. Kim, having just walked up, noticed the exchange and immediately reached into his pocket and pulled out the money they had paid him just a few minutes previously.

"We will send this back to you just as soon as we have settled in Vienna. I am so sorry, my friend. I have been away for so long that I didn't think of rates being as high as they are now," Ling confessed.

"It is no problem. I had to fly cargo here anyway. Keep the money as a gift of friendship and a blessing for both of us from the Lord," offered Kim.

With a handshake and farewell, Kim left Ling and Allen to wait their afternoon flight. The flight was fully boarded and the engines whined as the Soviet Ilyushin Il-18 took off. Apprehension set in again as they were launched into another unknown. But God had cared for their safety many times and had even opened doors for them on their journey out of the mountainous country in South Asia.

The two used the flying time to sleep on the four hour flight to Hungary and again during the three hours to Vienna. As the plane descended over the Danube River, the second longest river in Europe, the two men witnessed beautiful views. As they landed in Vienna, the lush uninhabited mountains of Laos were replaced by thousands of people living among the most beautiful architecture in the world.

They gathered their luggage and headed toward customs with little fear. Up till now there had been no complications, but they couldn't help thinking this might be the one. Being an American and Chinese traveling pair with passports from a communist country could certainly create suspicion.

Again, however, they were ushered on through. As they cleared customs and found a quiet place away from the crowd they took a moment to breathe a sigh of relief.

Dr. Malin had corresponded with his friend, Karl, here in Vienna, and Allen and Ling knew he was going to meet and help them when they entered the city. Allen found a phone with the hopes that the number he had was still a working number. He was surprised when a voice speaking German answered.

"I can only speak English," Allen replied.

The next words he heard were more understandable. "Who is this?"

"I am Paul Rasmussen. Is this Mr. Karl Brendel?" Allen asked.

"Yes, oh yes. Malin advised me of your coming. I will be so glad to have you. Where are you now?" he questioned.

"We are at the Vienna International Airport. We have just arrived and gotten our luggage. Would you be so kind as to pick us up?"

"Give me your gate number and I will be there in forty-five minutes. If I remember Malin correctly, one of you is Caucasian and the other Oriental?"

"Yes, sir," replied Allen. "We will be anxious to meet you."

Hanging up the phone, relief washed over Allen. He and Ling found a bench close to their gate and bowed their heads together in prayer. The tears that could be seen on their cheeks were pure joy. They offered a series of praises remembering the many days of hard travel and thanking God for all His mercies. They knew they were in a city where they had never been and in a few minutes would turn their lives over to a man they had never met, but they were comforted by the Lord's presence.

Almost forty-five minutes to the second Karl arrived. He jumped out of his car and approached Allen and Ling. He greeted them with the exuberance of meeting long lost friends.

"You are Paul Rasmussen and Ling Kai," he stated in confirmation rather than asking.

"Yes sir, but if you please, I go by Allen, my middle name."

"Fair enough," Karl continued. "Malin gave me a good amount of information on you both. I'm looking forward to getting better acquainted."

The normal chatter between people riding in a car was infected by the joy of the two men meeting a new brother and tempered with the feeling of safety.

They were taken aback when they arrived at Karl's home. It was hard to compare such luxury with their humble home at Friendship Mission. Karl's home was a multi-leveled home with a number of apartments. It was located in a well kept neighborhood and not even back in the States had Allen stayed in such a place.

Karl reassured them, "This is my home and what is mine is yours. Since Malin told me you were coming to Vienna, I prepared two rooms upstairs for you. Unlike Malin, I never found a beauty like he did, and I have only been married to my music. It's going to be nice having company around here again."

Allen and Ling looked at each and thought of yet another hurdle the Lord had helped them cross.

A New Friend Helps With His Music Desire

The next few days were ones of relaxation and settling for both travelers. For nearly a month they had traveled, so both body and minds were exhausted. Coming from one of the sparsest areas of the world, where unrest prevailed, to a bustling city of a million or more overwhelmed them. The villages of Asia and small towns of America were replaced with vistas they had never seen. Vienna was a city filled with huge, beautiful buildings, in architecture different than anywhere they had been.

Karl, who had explained he would continue his schedule with students and other business matters, gave his two new guests freedom to be as comfortable as possible.

After a couple days Karl, Allen and Ling were having espresso around the table when Karl said, "I'm free for the day. Are you ready to see Vienna yet?"

"I sure would like that. Wouldn't you Ling?" answered Allen.

Ling agreed and got up to get ready. He and Allen saw the attire of Karl and dressed accordingly. As they began their tour of this unique city Allen could see why Dr. Malin and Dr. Angelika enjoyed living there so much.

Karl intrigued Allen and Ling with the knowledge he had of Vienna. He spoke proudly in his touring voice, "Vienna is Austria's leading city and is its cultural, economic, and political center. Vienna lies in the very east of Austria and is close to the Czech Republic, Slovakia and Hungary.

"I came here to the university to study music because Mozart, Beethoven, Brahms, Strauss, and Schubert are just a few of the musical luminaries who lived in Vienna and many of the theaters are always playing their material. Would you like to go to a Mozart symphony tonight?" he suddenly asked.

"Wow! Would I? That would be a real thrill to me," Allen exclaimed.

"What about you Ling?"

Ling nodded his approval with a wide smile.

"Great," Karl boomed. "Because I have already purchased our tickets!" Allen couldn't help but wonder how many other surprises Karl would pull out of his sleeve.

Karl switched gears and returned to his tour guide voice again, "Besides musical halls, the Schönbrunn Palace in Vienna is one of the most important cultural monuments in Austria and since the 1860s has been one of the major attractions. The palace and gardens illustrate the tastes, interests and aspirations of successive Habsburg monarchs. In earlier times it served as summer residence to various Habsburg rulers." As they drove up to the palace the two had never seen such a huge building and was impressed as they entered to see the unimaginable. Inside the palace, they learned many interesting facts about the imperial family, while continuing to enjoy further aspects of Baroque culture with a relaxing stroll around the gardens.

They admired the magnificent apartments of Maria Theresa; her sitting rooms, bedroom and the parlor in which 6-year-old Mozart used to play for the Empress, as well as the parlors and apartments of the Imperial couple, Franz Joseph and Sissi.

The interior was filled with frescoed ceilings, crystal chandeliers, huge mirrors and gilded ornaments. They visited almost forty rooms, but learned they had seen less than three percent of the residence's 1441 rooms.

Both fellows stood in one place and simply let their eyes dance from one picture to another, amazed at the wealth and splendor. Karl broke through their wonder when he asked, "How would you like this for a summer home?"

Allen laughed and said, "I couldn't even afford the door to the foyer."

"We will see more sites later. Right now we need to get home to prepare for the symphony," Karl announced.

During the return trip the three talked about all they had experienced for the day, and Karl was all but brimming with the excitement of what they would further experience that evening.

Upon entering the house, Karl informed Allen and Ling, "I know you do not have any tuxedos, but I keep many sizes here for when my students do their recitals and performances. You will find them in the closet of the second floor hall."

The afternoon went quickly and all were ready to go at the appointed time. Neither Allen nor Ling had ever been to a presentation like they were about to see, and they were full of questions.

"Where is the symphony going to be performed?" Allen inquired.

"It will be at the Musikverein Symphony Hall. It is considered one of the best halls in the world. It has the most beautifully ornate auditorium, and its exquisite sound truly makes this a world class concert hall."

Allen and Ling followed Karl into the entrance of the building like shy little kids waiting the unexpected. The usher took the tickets and gestured them to fellow. As he opened the doors to the auditorium, a beautiful building was revealed to them. Chandeliers, tapestry, and gold braiding like they had never seen decorated the entire place. All they could say to themselves was that they could not believe it.

After being seated in prime box seats, they continued to observe everything around them. Karl broke into their amazement with more information, "This is going to be a Mozart Symphony and everyone will be dressed in the costumes of his era."

Karl's announcement didn't even dent their wonderment, as they were not sure what people dressed like during his time. In a few minutes artists with their instruments began to gather on the stage.

The dress was very unique with gold colored pants to their knees and white stocking to the shoes. The shirts matched and were full with a brown slash from shoulder to waist. The most stunning thing that Ling questioned was, "Why the white wigs?"

By now nearly 150 people had entered and were seated on the stage. Ling leaned over to Allen and whispered with a chuckle, "You know, those white wigs at this distance make me think of the cotton balls we cleaned within the clinic."

The man in the first chair of the violin section stood and walked to the front of the wind instruments. He placed his violin under his chin and lifting up his bow, pulled it down in one swift move. The chilling sound could be heard all across the hall and was quickly followed by blowing toots from the wind section.

He moved in front of the percussion section and did the same thing. This time a thunderous boom, Boom, BOOM! followed.

Finally, he came before the string section and again the screeching sound of his violin was heard. Screeching sounds from the violins and other string instruments started instantly.

He sat down, and the conductor entered the stage. The first thing he did was shake the hand of the man in the first chair. While the tuning period was disconcerting, the handshake puzzled the two strangers even more.

The concert lasted for almost two hours with Allen and Ling not missing a thing in the presentation. Before the next to last number, the conductor left the podium and disappeared behind the stage. Allen and Ling turned to each other with questioning looks when they noticed that every eye was directed toward the man in the first chair again.

As before, he lifted his bow and as he pulled it down the entire orchestra began at the same time with him.

Allen turned to Ling and commented, "They don't need a conductor at all."

Ling shook his head in agreement, "The man in the first chair does it all."

Before the conclusion of the concert, the conductor returned and clicked his baton on the podium three times. As he came down the last time, the presentation of that music was beyond their imagination. They had never heard music like it.

All the way home Karl answered question after question from the two curious younger men, including the reason for the white wigs.

"Fellows, I brought you to the symphony tonight not only for your enjoyment, but to search out your needs. Allen, it is apparent that I have a lot of work to do if this is the area you wish to pursue," Karl revealed.

His Accomplishment Rewarded

Allen and Ling welcomed every new experience Karl offered them, but knew they needed to get settled into a routine. Ling had had a long talk with Allen and decided he wanted to stay in Austria. He was enjoying the city and all he could learn from being there. Since he had not come to Austria to train as a pianist, he found a job to support his needs at the University Hospital, but continued on at the Brendel home and offered his assistance to his friends.

It was not long until Ling found he could get credit from working as a nurse in training, so he began taking classes as well. He didn't think he would ever get the opportunity to go to college. He certainly hadn't come to Austria with the thought in mind, but he was overjoyed with the opportunity to better himself.

Ling wrote home to his brothers every week, and after a short period of time, he was able to send them money to continue helping support them. He knew that Lang had established himself in a medical clinic and was supporting himself, and that Noi was finishing school, but Ling would always feel responsible for his brothers.

Allen, on the other hand, had come to be taught by Karl Brendel whose experience and knowledge of music was renowned. He and Karl began music studies and practiced on a regular basis in the studio in Karl's home.

It became apparent to Allen that Karl was giving much more time and attention to him than to his other students, and he assumed it was because of the commitment he had made to Dr. Malin. Karl, however, was quite interested in the fact that Allen was already a good pianist, but knew he could only become better by understanding the diverse methods presented in classical music.

The days and weeks that followed were much the same. The mornings were filled with learning theories, and the afternoon hours were spent practicing. Mozart, Beethoven, Brahms, Strauss, and Schubert were all part of the curriculum designed by Karl Brendel.

Allen was finding the work harder than he expected, but very rewarding.

Karl, a master pianist himself, was patient with Allen's simple mistakes.

He corrected Allen when necessary, but was also quick to praise when he did well.

Karl was well known in the city, and his friendships with renowned musicians were limitless. He began to compare Allen with another young pianist who had a similar introduction to the higher classics. He began to relate the successes of them both to build confidence in Allen.

"Alfred Fisher was a great piano player," he started. "He came from a nonmusical family, just like you Allen. He became a widely regarded classical pianist and was acknowledged by some as the best. He really could play Schumann and Brahms. I sometimes thought he was even better than they, and all without a formal music education. Ah, so much like you, I can't overcome the similarity. You continue as you are, and you will be good one day I believe."

Day after day for eight years Allen had trained intensely under a master and had become quite proficient. He had played many small recitals around Vienna, but now his intense training was about to pay off.

Karl alerted Allen by saying, "One of Austria's better pianists is playing in one of the lesser concert halls next month, and he asked if I knew someone that could open the program for him. 'Of course I do!' I told him with confidence.

"This artist is very temperamental and refuses to play with those that intimidate him, but you will teach him a lesson or two," Karl chuckled as he walked into the parlor for afternoon tea.

Following after him an ecstatic Allen asked, "Do you believe I am ready?"

"You would never have gotten the opportunity if I had thought otherwise," Karl chided him.

"I have great confidence in you and know you would never put me on stage before you knew I was capable. This is the day for which I have been waiting. Thank you, Professor Brendel," Allen acknowledged with excitement.

Allen's apprehension began to lesson with daily practice. Karl had gotten him permission to use the concern hall when there was not a performance so that he could have the feeling of playing before others.

On the night of the concert Karl left early with Allen for the concert hall so he could get the feel and hear the sound of the hundreds who were in attendance. Karl kept encouraging Allen as they sat backstage waiting for his first performance before such a crowd.

Allen was very nervous, but confident he would do well. The moisture in his hands was obvious, and he kept wiping them with a handkerchief that Karl had given him. He rose and began to walk while saying a brief prayer. He knew God would support him and enable him to perform as he had practiced for the evening.

Allen had no idea his breakthrough would come that night as he played one of the most famous of piano concertos, the Fourth Concerto written by Beethoven.

The press the next day published, "Who is this new Beethoven? Brendel has found us another."

Allen was fast becoming one of the most thoughtful interpreters of classical Germanic works. His favorite composers became Beethoven, Schubert, and Mozart. He was reluctant to play under his new name, Paul Allen Rasmussen, and so decided to honor his teacher and favorite composers by playing under the name Karl Beetschuzart.

Allen's feelings were very much a part of his musical presentation and one could sense his emotion and love for the music. He did not want people to think he was showing off his ability, he just wanted others to feel what he felt.

Becoming a well known pianist under a pseudonym was trying at times. Allen was still concerned that others would be suspicious of who he really was, but he was not willing to give up what he had to go back to the United States with the truth. Allen need not have worried because people forgot their questions about his identity as soon as they heard his first song.

Ling had spent his eight years in nurse's training and had gained a lot of confidence in the medical field while earning his Master's Degree in nursing. Because of his friendship with Allen, Ling willingly quit his job and joined Allen as his personal assistant while he traveled Europe and other countries of the world playing in known concert halls.

Allen and Ling quickly learned how hard it was to rush from city to city playing before different audiences and keeping up with the pace they had to keep, but they were enjoying all the new places of the world, and their friendship was being cemented even deeper.

Allen knew he owed his life to Friendship Mission, so he sent his total honorariums after expenses designated to the children's training at the compound. He had become so wrapped up in his music that he very seldom thought of the life he had tried to forget for so many years. It was in Toronto, Canada that what Allen used to fear most, happened.

After the performance, a gentleman gained permission to meet Allen. Shaking Allen's hand he commented, "You certainly look like someone from my past. Are you by chance Lieutenant Allen Livingston?"

Ling, standing off to the side, froze and stared in horror. Allen could only stare at the man and give no response.

"I can understand your reluctance to answer me, but let me tell you who I am. I am Captain John McIntosh, and I believe we served together at Kelly Air Force Base about twenty years ago. I know that Allen was classified a traitor by his country, but a year and a half, almost two years ago there was an article in the Military Post that the Air Force Commander had learned the truth of his accident, and they have been seeking his whereabouts. So I ask again. Are you Lieutenant Allen Livingston?"

By the end of Captain McIntosh's speech, Ling was by Allen's side and could hardly stand still for the excitement welling up within him. Allen, on the other hand, was finding the information hard to believe. Something within him told him to trust Captain McIntosh, so he answered, "Yes, I am Allen Livingston, and you and I did serve together at Kelly Air Force Base."

"Allen, you are a free man," yelled Ling. "Praise the Lord!" He grabbed Allen and hugged him fiercely. "Free, my friend."

"Yes, Ling. Can you believe it after all these years? God is certainly faithful." Allen then turned to Captain McIntosh, "You have made me happy to be an American again. I have been so hurt and confused since my crash behind enemy lines. What joy you have brought me!" he stated with tears in his eyes.

"There is more that I would like to share with you. Would you and your friend accompany my wife and me to dinner?" he asked.

Allen agreed that he and Ling would join them for dinner. While Captain McIntosh's wife called a restaurant to make a reservation, he informed them that they were staying in a vacation home for the month and was so glad they had decided on seeing the performance.

After arriving at the fancy restaurant they were seated immediately. They ordered their meals and as they waited Captain McIntosh handed a folded paper to Allen.

"You may think it strange that I have kept this in my glove box all this time, but I just couldn't ever believe that you were a deserter, and when I read this article about the truth, I hung onto it."

Allen held the article so that he and Ling could read at the same time. As he read the liberating news, he was awe-struck by the information given:

Two years ago the Commander learned that the theory of Lieutenant Sam Cunningham lying about Lieutenant Allen Livingston leaving his post and deserting his country was true. Further investigation, with the help of Prince Souva Phuma and Dr. Malin Rasmussen in Laos, uncovered the wreckage of Lt. Livingston's plane this past year. The investigation has been finalized and all charges against Livingston have been dropped. If anyone knows his whereabouts, the Commander asks to be advised.

"Dr. Malin knew," stated Allen. "Ling, why don't you think he ever contacted me?"

"I'm sure that Dr. Malin had a very good reason. You must not hold any ill feelings toward him until you know for certain what his reason was," Ling advised.

Turning to Captain McIntosh Allen asked, "Have you any idea why Cunningham would have lied about me? I know he didn't like me being a Christian, but . . ."

"I don't know what made him do it," commented McIntosh. "I recently heard from both Brogan and Grissom and they share the same story. They said that right after your plane went down Cunningham headed back to base. At the debriefing session, he was irate and blamed you for leaving him unprotected and then said he saw you fly away with the enemy. He swore that you were a traitor and signed the papers. Shortly after that, Grissom said that Cunningham started going to church on occasions and shared that he had been a preacher's kid but had gotten hurt at how a church treated his father. The squadron was split up after a year or so. Grissom and Brogan were transferred back to California, and Cunningham stayed in Thailand as a wing man for another unit. His plane was shot down and right before he died he confessed to the chaplain that he had lied about you, and he asked forgiveness. The military, at the time, was so wrapped up in the war, that they didn't take time to really investigate the situation. They blew it off and said that Cunningham was probably traumatized since he was on his deathbed. I don't know what reopened the investigation, but I'm thankful for the outcome."

"You can't be any more thankful than I am," laughed Allen. "But tell me, you have talked with Brogan and Grissom?"

"Yes, both are retired now. Brogan lives back in Conway, Arkansas where he has a small farm. He told me he enjoys fishing in the area lakes called Beaverfork and Conway. Grissom lives in Farmington, Missouri where he says he spends his time hunting. He and his wife enjoy shows at the Fox Theater in St. Louis. I have both their addresses if you want them," McIntosh said.

Finishing dinner with the captain and his wife was very pleasant. Since this was the last stop on Allen's latest tour, McIntosh asked if he and Ling would stay a couple days and enjoy their vacation home. "I'm sure you could use some relaxing after all that has happened today. We probably won't be able to contact the Commander till after the weekend anyway, and then it's going to take several days for anything to happen at the Pentagon," McIntosh assured them. "Come stay with us a couple days before you return to Austria."

His Life Takes A Change

Allen and Ling spent four days with Captain McIntosh. The first two days they went on a fishing trip about 100 miles east of Toronto at RiceLake north of Colborg. They fished both days catching Northern Pike and Yellow Perch. Their days ended with fish fries at the cabin they had rented.

Ling, laughing as he ate, told the other two, "Now fellows, this is the life!"

The drive back to the McIntosh's home was peaceful and enjoyable for Allen. For the first time in years he felt relieved from the pressures that had harassed him.

As they drove west down the Queens highway, he glanced toward the left of the highway and viewed the large expanse of LakeOntario and thought how there would be no more gulf between him and an opportunity to return back to his American homeland. He wanted to stop and call his parents, but he feared doing that until the Pentagon assured him that he would not be charged.

After two more days visiting in the area around Canada's largest city, Allen and Ling had to return to Austria. Allen still wondered if the good news was a dream.

He had received a call from the commandant who assured him that a deeper investigation had indeed shown they made a mistake and his records had been erased of his being called a traitor or AWOL for the years in question. The rest of the details to get him back to the States were being finalized and they would be in touch with him.

Allen offered his Austrian address and phone number, "Someone will have to contact me there. I still have obligations that I must fulfill."

The British Airways flight roared as it left the ground at 10 p.m. Soon the lights were dimmed and a movie was started. The film entitled "Is All Well Back Home?" began to play.

Ling turned to Allen, "What a title to start a trip home," he chuckled.

"But Allen, Vienna is really not home to me, nor is China," he whispered sadly. "Friendship Mission is my home. I miss Dr. Rasmussen and so many of the others there. I wonder how things are."

Allen looked at Ling with a humored expression and said teasingly, "I bet one of the 'others' is Song Soo. Now don't tell me a lie."

Ling was one of the most honest and trustworthy men Allen had ever met and he wished he had not teased Ling that way. However, Ling surprised Allen with, "Yes, I have thought of her many times since we have been away, but I doubt she has given much thought to me."

"I think I will call Dr. Malin when we get back to Vienna. Do you want me to ask him about Song Soo for you?" asked Allen humoring Ling.

"No! No, don't embarrass me," Ling pled.

The movie concluded and the lights were turned off. Most of the passengers had closed their eyes and were drifting off to sleep. The time of conversation with Allen caused Ling to begin thinking of times past and especially working with Song Soo.

In less than three hours the light began to peer into the interior of the plane. Flying east into the sun created a short night for the passengers, but it was even shorter for Ling, who had not slept at all.

The plane landed in about four hours at Heathrow airport near London. Due to a transfer of planes, they had about three hours of layover. They stopped in a coffee shop where the discussion started again.

"I noticed you didn't sleep any last night," Allen commented to Ling who was wiping his eyes.

"Well, I might have if you wouldn't have brought up Song Soo. She was all I could think about all night," Ling accused Allen with a blush.

As they boarded another British Airways flight to Vienna, Allen promised Ling he would not bring up the subject again. Ling returned a look of satisfaction, but said, "I don't believe you, Allen. You like to tease me too much!"

Then in an effort to get back at Allen, Ling asked, "Who do you dream about these days?"

"No one. I have gotten over the two I was ever attracted too, and God has not seen fit to provide His choice for me yet," Allen responded as he pushed back his seat hoping to go to sleep.

The three hour flight was uneventful and both were happy as the plane landed safely. They gathered their luggage and called Karl to come get them as had become their custom while traveling.

It was always a reunion when Karl arrived. He ran from the car and hugged them before loading their belongings and heading for home. During the ride Allen told Karl about what had happened while in Canada. He had never talked to Karl about his real identity and was surprised to learn that he already knew.

"Malin did not want me to be blind to what had happened in your life, and to what could have possibly happened to me if you were ever found in my house. Your secret has obviously been safe with me," Karl chuckled. "So when do you get to return home?"

"I am still waiting on a call from Washington, D.C." admitted Allen. "I'm quite sure Dr. Malin had a hand in the military finding out the truth. Do you have any idea why he would have never contacted me?"

"I'm sure, knowing Malin, that he had a very good reason for not telling you," said Karl. "Why don't you call him today?"

Allen relaxed only briefly before calling Dr. Malin. He dialed the long distance number and was surprised when Song Soo answered the phone. Dr. Malin had written several years before to tell Allen and Ling that Song Soo had committed her life to Jesus.

"How are you my precious sister?" he asked.

"Allen?

"Allen is that you?" she questioned.

"Yes, it is me. Allen Livingston," he said laughing. It felt so good to use his real name again. "How are you?"

"I am doing fine. We are all keeping busy. Dr. Malin is right here and wants to talk to you."

"Allen?

"Allen, can you hear me?" the kind doctor shouted.

"Yes, I can. Ling and I give our greetings to you and everyone there.

"How are you? Is your health okay?" Allen questioned.

"Allen, I'm getting old, but my health is fairly good for my age. I sure miss you and Ling. I think of you often, my boy, especially when I visit Angelika and the children. Thank you again for helping me to be assured that I would see them again in Heaven. This has made my loneliness easier," he whispered sadly.

"I think I need to thank you for making my loneliness easier too," said Allen. "I have just recently been told that the United States has learned the truth about my plane crash. Your name was given in a news article I read. Why didn't you ever tell me?"

"Because, Jonah, you had to live your own life like you wanted until the time God could work things out for you. He didn't want this meddling old man to get you out of the whale before it was time. I did what God asked of me, and let Him do what He needed to do for you. Do not be angry with me for that, my boy" pleaded Dr. Malin.

"I could never be angry with you Dr. Malin. I just needed to know your reason. But what do you mean by meddling? What is it you actually did?" questioned Allen.

"Four years ago there was a group of men who were doing some forestry work close to the compound. I found out they had uncovered your wreckage, and I didn't want them to mess with it. I knew that was your only chance of redemption from your country. I didn't know what to do to stop the group, so I did what Angelika would have done. I prayed. The Lord told me to go to Princess Ping. She and Prince Phuma were able to stop the forestry work in that immediate area, but they didn't know for how long. We decided it would be best to contact your government about the wreckage. The Lord, however, told me to keep my mouth shut. He knew the two of you would need to finish this portion of your life without me," Dr. Malin finished.

"My life will never be finished without seeing you again, old meddling man. I will be going back to the United States, but as soon as I can I will be coming to see you. I love you so much Dr. Malin, and I will never forget our close relationship. You are right. Only God could have made all this possible. I have been rethinking the calling He gave me when I was in high school. These years have been a paradox for me. The struggles He allowed, making my life miserable, and the directions He gave helped me to meet you, Ling, Ping, and others. God used you all to ease the pain of my grief. Now God is using you to bring me back to the goals I had once hoped to reach by being a minister of the Gospel. Thank you so much! May God continue to use you to bless others! May I talk to Song Soo again?"

"Hello! This is Song Soo. Allen, are you still on the line?"

"Yes, I am here. Do you miss us as much as we miss you? Would you like to see us again?"

"Wait! Just ask one question at a time. Let me answer with Yes! Yes! I really miss working with Ling. He was so kind and gracious to me. He made me feel so comfortable in a strange land when I first arrived at the compound," she related.

"I will tell him what you said," Allen offered.

"No! He might take it the wrong way. Oriental women are not supposed to reveal their feelings," she quickly said.

"Okay! I must go. Would you like to say something to Ling first?"

Pausing for only a moment she agreed that she would like to speak to him.

Allen handed the phone to Ling and said with a grin and wink, "Song Soo wants to talk to you."

Ling took the receiver from Allen and while placing it to his ear he punched Allen in the arm. He listened carefully to see if Song Soo was really there.

"Song Soo, this is Ling. How are you?"   "I miss you, Ling!" she blurted out.

"Oh, I'm so sorry!" In a much more reserved voice she said, "I am fine. I was not prepared to hear from you both today, and I am very excited. When will you be coming back to Friendship Mission?"

"As soon as I possibly can. I will be going with Allen to the United States, but soon after that trip I pray."

The phone line began wavering, but Ling caught Song Soo's last words, "I look forward to seeing you again," before the connection was lost.

Ling looked over at Allen and burst out loudly, "Wow! I think she likes me."

Allen spent the next few days putting his affairs in order so that he might leave Austria. His time in that country had been prosperous, but he knew it was only a third home after his United States and Friendship Mission. He and Ling spent time visiting and saying goodbye to friends that had been made before they had begun touring.

One evening as they rested, Allen told Karl and Ling, "You know, I can see why Dr. Malin loved this place."

Karl replied, "Malin loved this city more because it was where he found the love of his life."

Going Home After So Long

Allen was awakened one morning by Ling, "A telegram for you," he sang.

The telegram came from the Secretary of the Air Force. It gave his apology for the mistaken belief. The telegram was brief, and even though Allen easily memorized it, he read it again and again. Kissing the telegram and dancing around he said, "I wish I had a picture frame. I would frame this message. It is worth more than gold to me."

With that thought in mind, Allen was reminded of an old hymn. The joy and excitement he was feeling was so strong that he went to the piano to let his emotions flow the best way he knew how. Sitting on the bench he began to play:

I'd rather have Jesus than silver or gold,
I'd rather be His than have riches untold;
I'd rather have Jesus than houses or lands,
I'd rather be led by His nail-pierced hand.
I'd rather have Jesus than men's applause,
I'd rather be faithful to His dear cause;
I'd rather have Jesus than world-wide fame,
I'd rather be true to His holy name.
He's fairer than lilies of rarest bloom,
He's sweeter than honey from out the comb;
He's all that my hungering spirit needs,
I'd rather have Jesus and let Him lead.

As Allen came to the chorus the conclusion rang loudly with the emotion he was noted for:

Than to be the king of a vast domain
Or be held in sin's dread sway;
I'd rather have Jesus than anything
This world affords today.

Suddenly his exuberant joy was replaced with tears. He knelt at the bench and convulsively prayed with thanksgiving and rejoicing. Ling, who had been listening from his supportive spot in the corner, held Allen and praised the Lord with him.

The next day the President of the United States sent a telegram advising that Allen would be receiving a Medal of Honor and gave him an invitation to the White House. He was to be in Washington D.C. the day after tomorrow.

Once again Allen rejoiced and was complimented that the President would contact him. "What an honor," he thought.

After nine years in the compound with Dr. Malin and ten more years outside of the United States, he was finally going home. He realized that he was suddenly nervous about returning to his home country. He wondered what kind of a reception he would actually receive.

Allen and Ling boarded the plane in Vienna, Austria to begin the flight to the United States. Allen had only dreamed this would ever happen, but somehow never lost hope that the truth would be discovered.

Professor Karl Brendel, in whose house they had lived for nearly ten years, was seen to be weeping joyful tears for Allen and Ling as he waved during their departure. He had left those two at the airport where he had picked them up many times over the past several years. As he made this final walk back to his car he whispered a prayer of thanksgiving to the Caring Father.

The flight from Vienna would stop at Heathrow Airport in London where Allen and Ling would change planes. The trip had been very smooth and uneventful until it began to cross the English Channel near Osteen, Belgium. There they were able to see many beautiful sights from their window.

They viewed a hovercraft and a hydroplane. They also saw a large ferry ship just leaving from Dover, with the White Cliffs glistening in the bright sunlight.

Allen turned to Ling and said, "The White Cliffs of Dover are world-famous. They have been of major historical importance for generations, being scarred with defenses and fortifications from countless wars. The dominant feature on the Cliffs is Dover Castle, which began life as an Iron Age hill fort defending the town from invaders.

"This site has seen many changes from the Roman Empire to the Second World War. After the Battle of Hastings, William the Conqueror rebuilt the Norman Keep."

As the two continued their sightseeing, a scripture came to Allen. He shared with Ling, "White is usually a symbol of purity and cleanliness. Revelation 2:17 says, *'To him who overcomes I will give some of the hidden manna to eat. And I will give him a white stone, and on the stone a new name written which no one knows except him who receives it.'"*

They had viewed the Cliffs for miles as the plane began to make its descent into London. The landing was smooth and deplaning was easy. They had very little time before they were to board the plane for New York City.

Since their next flight was heading straight into the west wind, the plane was quite bouncy in the rough turbulence. Allen and Ling both held tightly to their seat and knew if they took their seatbelts off their heads would hit the ceiling. The strong head winds were so forceful and continuous they were ready to land long before the ten hour flight ended.

As the plane was finally descending to land at the large airport in New York, Allen saw first an object that flooded his eyes with tears: The Statue of Liberty.

She had been a symbol of freedom for Allen long before he made his pledge to defend his country. He thought of all the immigrants who had seen these same shores, and he suddenly felt like one of them. The words of Emma Lazarus' poem, engraved on the base of the Statue of Liberty, came to his mind: *"Give me your tired, your poor, your huddled masses yearning to breathe free."* Allen knew he was getting ready to breathe free again.

Allen and Ling quickly found the gate to board their plane to Washington D.C. They had hardly gotten airborne when their descent toward the National Airport began. As the plane taxied to its assigned gate, the stewardess announced, "Please stay seated, and I will advise you when you may deplane. Mister Allen Livingston and Mister Ling Kai, would you please come forward."

They retrieved their small bags from the overhead bins and started toward the front. "Please wait here," she commanded.

The door of the plane was opened and four uniformed military personnel advanced toward them. Allen and Ling were told by the officer in charge that he needed to see their passports. Ling immediately gave the officer his, but Allen began to dig in the outside pocket of his bag.

"My passport Sir, but I think these will prove also that I am Allen Livingston," he said as he offered his dog tags to the officer.

Allen was stunned as countless reporters were positioned to photograph and listen to the welcome by the spokesman for the President.

"I want to welcome back to our country a faithful servant of our military, Lieutenant Allen Livingston." The crowd began wildly applauding and cheering, but before the spokesman could continue with his planned speech, even louder shouts were heard as Mr. and Mrs. Livingston broke through the four uniformed men and engulfed Allen in hugs, kisses, and tears of joy.

The men assigned to Allen had met his parents, so they knew this interruption was not a threat to him, and while they were supposed to wait for all protocol, decided to let the family continue with their reunion.

Finally, the officer in charge stepped in, "Sir, we must finish with the proceedings." He had Allen's parents step aside so the spokesman could finish his introduction of Allen.

Allen was not used to such attention and was quite uncomfortable getting all the accolades from the military and media.

Soon enough the meeting was over and Allen found himself being whisked by the four military men down a crowded hallway.

The Secret Service had previously checked him into a hotel and entered through a private entrance on a floor available only to Allen and the men assigned to be his escort and protection.

While Allen was being settled into his room, he asked about his parents. The Secret Service, he was told, had decided for all purposes of safety to house his parents in a different location. The agent offered no further explanation or information.

Allen desperately wanted to talk to them. He knew they had been thrilled to see him again, but he had also seen the pain in their eyes. He had so much to try and explain to them, and he didn't want to wait any longer than necessary.

With an audible sigh Allen resigned himself to the situation and realizing how tired he was began to prepare for bed. While doing so the phone rang. He had hopes it was his parents, but the Secret Service agent from the sitting area said, "The President is on the phone. You may pick it up in your room."

Allen, slightly taken aback, answered the phone, "This is Allen Livingston."

The President began, "Lieutenant Livingston how was your trip from Austria?"

"It was a long flight," Allen admitted, "but I am happy to be back home."

"I want to apologize again for what has been done to you. Our country will try and make it up to you in a ceremony tomorrow morning. Are the accommodations fine?" "Yes, thank you, Mr. President. I am fine."

"If you have any needs, the men with you have been authorized to see to it that you are comfortable and safe," said the Commander-in-Chief.

"I appreciate their being with me and taking care of my needs. Again, I thank you, Sir," Allen concluded.

"Then I look forward to meeting you tomorrow, Lieutenant."

As they did every night before retiring, Allen and Ling bowed beside each other and thanked God for His blessings on them. Tonight Allen went to bed thanking God for the reconciliation and being back in the homeland he had pledged to protect.

As he drifted off to sleep, he wondered about the protocol and what would be involved the next day. He knew he could probably only imagine half of what was planned. He prayed that he would have the endurance to gain back his former life.

His Grief Turns To Honor

After rising from a sound sleep, Allen shaved and showered. As he returned to his bedroom the officer in charge entered the room. "Is there anything I can do for you this morning?"

Allen had stopped in his tracks as he stared at the brand new uniform laid out on the bed. "The rank isn't correct," he stated.

The assigned escort said, "The Secretary of the Air Force took into consideration the years you lost and has advanced your rank to a full Colonel. I am sure you will be recompensed for your lost pay and that it will be retroactive when everything else is determined."

"Wow!" Allen exclaimed. "It is hard to believe this is all happening to me. I was only doing what I was supposed to do for my country. Even with all the attention given me, I still don't feel worthy. Standing in front of everyone scares me, and I am afraid I will do the wrong thing."

Allen knew the news media, military officers, and congressional officials would be there. He turned to the agent and asked, "What am I supposed to do as I meet all the high ranking people?"

The escort, a former military officer himself, replied with the question, "What would you have done years ago when you met an officer whose rank was higher than yours?"

"I would salute him," the new colonel answered.

"Well, you have the answer," the Secret Service agent smiled.

Allen was surprised to find the uniform fit him perfectly. The gold braid, ribbons, and medals were all neatly positioned. He had forgotten how he felt in a full dressed uniform. The style and colors had changed, but he felt well dressed and proud to be wearing them.

Ling gave a low whistle as he entered the room. "You look like a hero, my friend," he complimented. He was inspecting Allen's uniform when the escorts advised them they were prepared to leave.

The agents had put on fresh suits, armed themselves, and made sure their communication devices were working. The man in charge announced, "It is time to go." Then turning to Allen asked, "Are you ready, Sir?"

Allen nodded and answered, "Yes sir!"

In protected formation the escorts surrounded the honoree as they departed to a car waiting to take them to the presentation on the Capitol steps. As the car stopped, Allen, humbled by the large crowd of people, began to tremble. Again the men surrounded him and began their walk to the platform.

Allen immediately saw the President of the country, the Vice-President, the Secretary of the Air Force, and other high ranking men on the platform. As he advanced to the first step he stopped, looked straight at the President, became completely erect, and raised his hand in a snapping salute. Turning toward the flag he again performed another salute of allegiance.

Oblivious to the other people he walked with a military color guard to the seat designated for him. The military band was playing and some of the dignitaries prepared to give their opening remarks. Afterward, the President advanced to the podium and looked out with passionate eyes.

The president began, "There are times when we all make mistakes. There are times when men's knowledge is hampered by misinformation. We are gathered here today to make things right to a hero who gave nine years of his life in enemy territory, not able to return to a country he thought had betrayed him. Colonel Livingston, please come forward."

As Allen started forward, he was joined by the Secretary of the Air Force.

The President continued, "As Commander-in-Chief I want to apologize to you for our nation's wrong and have taken measures to assure you that any records to the contrary are corrected. I wish to honor you with this Medal for your service."

The crowd of people all stood, clapping and cheering,

Feeling so honored brought Allen near to tears. All of the bitter feelings he felt in South Asia had melted away. The Secretary stood to the side as the President stepped toward Allen and placed the ribbon around his neck. The three saluted each other as the reporters and photographers moved swiftly around the front of the platform.

Then the President announced, "We have not come here just for a ceremony. We have come here to make amends. Therefore, I want to have Chaplain Andy Raines who you knew in Udorn, Thailand to come and ask our Lord to forgive all our trespasses and grief you have had."

Chaplain Raines glanced at Allen with a timid smile then prayed.

"O Lord, Lover of men, who forgives us our sins; cleanse us of all that is base or selfish, and make us to be in all things thy servants, and the messengers of thy love.

"Grant, O Lord, that we may meet all difficulties and temptations with a stedfast heart, in the strength of thy indwelling spirit.

"Shield us, O God, from the darkness of soul which sees thee not, and from the loneliness of heart which hears not thy voice, and through life and in the valley of the shadow of death, forsake us not; for thy Name's sake.

"Deepen and quicken in us, O God, a sense of thy Presence, and make us to know and feel that thou art more ready to teach and to give than we to ask or to learn; through Jesus Christ our Lord.

"O most merciful Redeemer, Friend, and Brother.
"May I know thee more clearly.
"May I love thee more dearly.
"May I follow thee more nearly.
Amen."

When the press withdrew a short distance, the Secretary of the Air Force advanced to the podium and said, "We are grateful you have all come and shared with us the honor that has been bestowed on another of our heroes. You are dismissed."

Many of the officers and officials made their way to Colonel Livingston and shook his hand. As the crowd slowly left Allen saw a small group that remained at the back of the seating area. He knew Ling and his parents were a part of the group, but it wasn't until he got closer that he recognized his sister, Beverly.

"Allen!" she yelled and ran into his arms. While she repeatedly hugged him she started ranting as only a sister can, "The Air Force sent us a telegram saying you had rejected the United States, but we didn't believe it for one minute! We did think for many years that you must be dead. We never once heard from you. You better start explaining."

By the end of her tirade she was alternating between shaking her finger in Allen's face and putting her hands on her hips in a very stern manner.

Allen's dad stepped into the moment, "Beverly, we all have questions that need to be answered, but for now we need to be content on having our Allen home with us."

"You are right, Dad," she said while backing off, "but this isn't over," she told Allen pointing her finger at him one last time. Allen chuckled and turned to see who the other four men standing in the group were. He began tearing up again as he recognized his former squad members.

The first two to greet him were Brogan and Grissom. Then Captain Nichols and Colonel Glenn moved toward him. After embracing each one, Allen said, "I want to thank you for standing with me and believing in me."

Colonel Glenn immediately said, "I am so sorry I listened to Cunningham above the others. I knew in my heart it couldn't be right, but I followed just the facts that I could find at the time. I was certainly wrong, and I apologize again."

"We are so sorry it took so long for the truth to finally surface," Brogan said. "Grissom and I tried several times to get the case opened, but we always hit roadblocks."

"It's something that Cunningham made a decision for Christ before he died. If he wouldn't have done that, we may have never found you," added Grissom.

"I guess that's the one bright star shining through those dark years I had.

Because of what I suffered there is another soul in Heaven today," commented Allen. "And now let me introduce you to the man who saved my life."

Allen motioned for Ling, having been standing away from the group, to join him. "Gentlemen, this is Ling Kai. He rescued me from the wreckage, gave his blood so I could live, and has helped me in all my endeavors since the day I was shot down," Allen proudly said.

Allen was introduced to his friends' wives and the group remained talking for several more minutes. Each of them would be attending the banquet in Allen's honor later that evening, and as the Secret Service agents were still on guard over Allen, the group disbanded till then.

Before walking away, Brogan handed Allen a piece of paper. "We have all written down our addresses so you can keep in touch. It sure is good to see you again, Buddy."

As Allen was riding to the banquet facility, he replayed the earlier events in his mind. He thought of the goodness bestowed him, and remembered one of his favorite childhood verses: Galatians 5:13 *"For you, brethren, have been called to liberty; only do not use liberty as an opportunity for the flesh, but through love serve one another."*

It Was Worth The Wait

Allen's parents and Beverly went back to Arkansas while Allen stayed in Washington D.C. for several days of meetings. Finally he and Ling boarded a plane for Little Rock. Allen raised his head and slowly opened his tear-filled eyes after a brief, but sincere prayer and said, "I'm going home. After twenty years I'm going home."

Suddenly his life verse from Genesis 33: 12 came to mind: *"Let us take our journey; let us go, and I will go before you."* Allen's pride was shattered as he cried, trying to protect his privacy.

The little Oriental man sitting next to him had been away from home even longer; except for the few days when they visited his uncle and left his brothers. Ling had never enjoyed the benefits Allen had.

"Ling, I have no closer friend than you. We have a common bond that few have ever had. I have always considered you a soul mate, and you have never let me down. I am going home to family and friends, and I am excited. Do you ever want to go to China to live again?" Allen inquired.

"I feel toward you as you do me. You are the only real family I have except Lang, Noi, and my uncle, but I was never close to him," Ling quietly responded with obvious tears. "I do not long to go back to China. My longing is for Friendship Mission. That is where my heart is now," he confided.

David and Martha Livingston had always hoped Allen was alive, but had little assurance that it was possible. When the rumors started circulating four years previously that Allen's disappearance was not due to desertion, their hope had been refreshed yet again. When they learned that the wreckage of his plane was found, their world came crashing down until several weeks later they had a report that his life had been saved in a mission compound behind enemy lines. They continued to pray daily for him as they had promised Allen in the very beginning. Their prayers were answered when the telegram arrived from the Pentagon that Allen was alive and would be coming home.

They now waited patiently in the airport for his arrival. The town of Little Rock had turned out in great numbers to show their local hero their support. There was very few who knew Allen that actually believed he could be a deserter, and all wanted to show how important he was to their community.

As Allen and Ling left the terminal they first heard the cheering crowd and then saw the many with signs and banners welcoming him home. The mayor and governor were there to meet him also, and welcomed him, Ling, and his parents a ride in a limousine to their home in Conway.

Allen couldn't help but notice the many police and military cars outside the airport. As the limousine pulled away, the other vehicles fell in line before and after to create quite a procession. They didn't take Allen straight home, but instead drove him straight through downtown where all the businesses had placed their flags on the sidewalks and the rest of the community's citizens lined the streets to wave and cheer their hero.

The car stopped in front of the court house square. The mayor of Conway told Allen that the city had something special to share with him. As the Livingston family and Ling joined the mayor on the court house steps the local high school band played.

The mayor approached a microphone and addressed the crowd, "My fellow citizens, let us welcome our hometown hero, Colonel Allen Livingston back to Conway, Arkansas." The cheers were so loud the mayor had to wait before he could continue.

"In honor of the service you have provided your country, and with great pride from your hometown, we give you this key to our city." The mayor shook Allen's hand and then addressed the waiting crowd again.

"I know many of you will want to shake Colonel Livingston's

hand, but we know how tired he is and would like for him to have a few days rest. I also know from personally speaking with his parents that they would love some quiet time with him. We would like Colonel Livingston and his family to have a little time to put their lives back in order before we add any more chaos. On Friday night we will have a party to honor and recognize Colonel Livingston and everyone is invited. This event will be held at the Dexter College auditorium and the doors will open at 6 p.m. We are hoping to convince the Colonel to play some of that classical music we have been hearing about. What do you say, Colonel?"

Allen overwhelmed with the activities of the day and the plans for three days later had a large smile on his face. "Yes," he agreed. "I will play for you."

As the crowd started shouting and applauding again, the mayor yelled, "Great!" He then more quietly said to Allen and his family, "Now into the car with you. The driver will see you safely to your house. Welcome home, Colonel. We will see you on Friday evening."

The crowd made way for Allen and his family to leave. He was relieved to finally be on his way home – to his house. He couldn't wait to walk through the front door and smell the familiarity of his childhood.

He was glad to see that well-wishers had left signs in his front yard, but there was no crowd gathered. He stepped from the car and soaked in his surroundings. While Ling helped the driver unload their bags, Mr. and Mrs. Livingston took their son's arms and led him into the house.

Once inside Allen melted into their arms and began to sob. The last twenty years were finally going to be released. By the time the three got their emotions under control Ling had carried in the bags and Beverly had arrived from the festivities in town.

"All right, Colonel," Beverly began. "Let's hear it."

"Everyone get comfortable, and I'll bring in the lemonade and cookies," suggested Mrs. Livingston.

"I'll help," Ling offered as he followed her to the kitchen.

"Beverly, I know you have been upset more than your mother and me," said Mr. Livingston. "We have discussed Allen's disappearance many times, and you know your mother and I feel that God was in control the whole time. Please don't turn this joyous occasion into a fight. Give Allen a chance to speak in peace."

Beverly began crying and as Mrs. Livingston and Ling carried the refreshments in a new wave of emotion overtook the family and it was several more minutes before anyone could speak. To Allen's surprise it was Ling, who was usually so quiet, who chose to speak first.

"I was working outside the mission compound's walls on the day Allen's plane was shot down. My brothers and I managed to get to him and move him to the clinic where Dr. Malin and Dr. Angelika saved his life. His leg was badly injured and had to have immediate surgery. He was very ill after that with fever, but the Lord kept His hand upon Allen. I was very fortunate to have gained a Christian friend."

Allen thought it strange that Ling's brief summarization ended with his testimony of friendship. He knew their friendship was a very special one, and only that morning they had talked about it on the plane, but he had never viewed God's plan from Ling's point of view before. Allen felt even more humbled by God's chosen path for his life.

"It was a long time before I could stand on my leg, and it took me months of physical therapy before I was strong enough to walk. During that time I found out that the United States had deemed me a traitor. I fell into a depression and didn't really care if I lived or died. I knew that I had turned my back on God's plan for my life by enlisting in the military to begin with, and I didn't care how He chose to punish me. I knew I deserved it, and I lost my will to fight."

"Oh, my poor baby," sobbed Allen's mother.

"Its okay Mom. Ling here wasn't going to let me give up so easily. He fed me scripture verses with breakfast each morning and thankfully the Lord hadn't given up on me either."   "We never gave up either, Son," Mr. Livingston said in a choked voice. "We prayed daily just like we told you we would. We knew that you would never have deserted, so we assumed that you must be a prisoner of war or maybe even dead. There were some very sad times over the years, but we never gave up our hope."

"Once I was strong enough that I could have left, I decided that it would be better for you to believe me dead and move on in life than to have to go through a court-martialing. The Lord gave me peace about that decision and even gave me a ministry in the compound," Allen told them.

"Well, truth be told," Beverly spoke again, "Mom, Dad and I got our own peace about your absence too. The Lord allowed us to see that whatever had happened or was happening to you was in His will for your life. We learned a lot about trusting the Lord over the past twenty years," she admitted.

The family continued talking late into the evening. They each tried to hit as many highlights from the years as they could. They shared laughter and more tears, but by bed time many hurts had been healed and understanding took place. The family was reunited in love, Allen was going to sleep in his own bed, and Ling felt like he really belonged.

After two days of rest Allen was ready to get out and see his old stomping grounds. Allen, Beverly, and Ling drove north to Greenbrier and east to Glenn town community where he showed Ling the old log house where he had been born.

They walked up the hill to an area called Slate Point. Allen told Ling he and his cousins would slide down the slick slate on boards when they were kids. "Getting up the slate hill wasn't as much fun as going down it, but it was worth the effort," he remembered.

After touring that area Beverly suggested they drive over the hill from where they were to Soda Valley. Ling was fascinated with what he was seeing, but reminded Allen of the time. "You must meet your public tonight," he joked.

Arriving early at Dexter College, Allen met up with John Netherland, his senior class president. John had been put in charge by the mayor and advised Allen that the high school, Dexter College, and the Log Cabin Democrat had heavily promoted his concert and party. KCON, the only radio station in town, he was told, was running spots every hour about the hometown boy who made good.

Allen and Ling decided that if Allen was going to play, he better play first. They knew once he started talking to people the time would get away from them.

John said, "I will be introducing you. What do you want me to say?"

"John, if you don't mind, let me just walk out and begin playing. That will make me most comfortable."

Allen played for almost thirty minutes. Ling would have never thought his music could get more emotional, but Allen poured his twenty year's sorrows and joys into that performance.

There were so many Allen would want to talk to that it was decided that he would give a brief speech from the stage in order to answer the general questions just once. He spoke for less than ten minutes, but used that time to let others know that his life had been a rough journey at times, but life was more than what he could make it. His life was more about what God does to make things easier to live with.

The Spark Ignites Again

Ellen Mabrey had listened with awe to Allen play the piano and then she sat and watched him move around the room for the next three hours. She never got her chance to meet him, and the night was winding down quickly. She had noticed, Ling, Allen's faithful friend was never far from his side. She decided to approach him.

"Would you please make sure I get to talk to Allen before he leaves?" she asked Ling.

Curious as to whom this beautiful woman was, Ling asked, "Why do you want to do this?"

"We grew up together, and I wanted the opportunity to speak personally to him," she said. The sincerity of her voice made Ling agree to the encounter. He managed to pull Allen away from the last of the lingering crowd and brought him to where Ellen had been sitting patiently waiting.

Seeing this beautiful woman stirred something from deep within Allen, but he couldn't immediately identify what it was. She rose with an elegant grace and dignity, walking toward him with hands outstretched.

"Allen, it's so good to see you again," she told him. The lilt of her voice brought him up short of reaching her. He was suddenly transported back in time to the living room of Helen's house, only it was not Helen he was visiting. It was the owner of that compassionate voice.

Ellen, having misunderstood the look of wonderment on Allen's face, dropped her hands and showing just a hint of disappointment said, "You don't remember who I am, do you?"

"There has been a lot of water under the bridge since I was here last," admitted Allen, "But one could never forget a flower as lovely as you, Ellen." He reached out and grasped her delicate hands in his.

Ling, having never heard Allen speak so poetically, laughed outright. Suddenly embarrassed he turned quickly to leave, but Allen stopped him.

"Ling, this is Helen Mabrey's twin sister, Ellen. Ellen, this is my best friend, Ling Kia."

Ling recognized Helen's name and a quiet prayer for his friend formed in his mind. He didn't want to see Allen hurt yet again. He would have liked to have told this mesmerizing woman that, but instead he chose to say, "It's nice to meet you."

"I was wondering if we could spend a few minutes together and catch up on our lives," Ellen told Allen.

"I would enjoy that, but I'm ready to get out of here," gestured Allen. "Is there a quiet café nearby?"

"Almost everything in this town still closes by ten, but I do know of a nice place in Little Rock that we can drive to if you are interested."

"Sounds great! Ling, will you join us?" Allen asked.

Ling, who was always in tune to Allen's needs said, "Not tonight Allen. Keeping up with you has worn me out. I think I'll catch a ride with your parents back to the house."

"Thanks, Ling. You're a trooper." Allen hugged his friend then turned to offer Ellen his arm. "Shall we?" he asked.

Looping her arm in his she answered, "We shall."

Watching the two of them leave could have caused a wave of jealousy to rise within Ling, but he was too aware of the bonding friendship he shared with Allen. On the contrary, he felt like he had known Ellen for all those years himself, and he welcomed an opportunity to befriend her as well.

Allen and Ellen sat across from each other in a corner booth at a nice little café. The waitress had brought their coffee, no cream, and warm apple pie a-la-mode. As they sat enjoying their treat, Allen realized that he had thought of Ellen on numerous occasions over the years.

"What are you thinking?" she quietly interrupted his thoughts.

"I was just realizing that you had crossed my thoughts many times over the past twenty years. You are even more attractive than I remembered."

"I always was the better looking twin," she joked.

"Not just that, but your demeanor. Your personality has always been attractive as well. I'm tired of talking about myself, as I'm sure you are tired of hearing about me. Please, tell me what you have done with your life."

"Well, after graduating from college in Oklahoma, I went to medical school at the University of Oklahoma. My studies were the normal courses for those wanting to practice medicine, but I wanted to specialize in tropical diseases and serve somewhere in a third world country. I took all the extra classes the curriculum offered and worked with researchers whose specialty was in that area.

"After four years of class and hospital training I went to Mayo Clinic in Rochester, Minnesota for additional training. I received excellent training during my residency to better qualify me to treat tropical diseases. I thought I was ready to serve the Lord in a medical mission hospital wherever my specialty was needed. My denomination, however, had no opening for a single, woman doctor, so my goal of serving God as a medical missionary didn't work out.

"Later I saw Baptist Hospital, here in Little Rock, needed a doctor in my specialty field, and I have worked there ever since."

"I'm impressed. I always knew you were full of compassion, and I'm sure you are a great asset to your profession." Allen knew of a great little mission work that could use Ellen, and he couldn't help but dream. His past history proved that he better not put the cart before the horse though.

The two spent the next several hours bringing each other up-to-date. Allen told her about his days in Laos and his love for Dr. Malin and Friendship Mission. He told of his love for Ping and how it ended in another heart break for him. "I still believe God must have the right person waiting for me."

Ellen looked deeply into Allen's eyes and said, "I still believe that same thing for myself. I was engaged once, but that ended, thankfully before a marriage."

She shook her head as if to clear her mind. "Allen, do you remember when you were dating Helen and had a flat on your car the morning of a date and again the next morning?"

Allen chuckled, "I had been broke for several days and couldn't understand the sudden testing of my already exhausted funds."

"You told Ellen, the next morning after the date, you had returned to the steering wheel and grasped it with tears when you spotted a five dollar bill.

"I never knew who it came from, but I thanked Helen for it," he remembered.

"I don't want to take anything away from your belief in her, but I left the five dollars," she confessed.

"You?" While Allen wasn't completely shocked, he was curious.

"I wanted you to come back at the end of the week, and I knew you couldn't unless I provided for you. I wasn't the one dating you, but always liked to be around you when you came to see Helen. She never wanted me around when you came because she sensed how I felt about you."

"You and I really were more compatible, but I was so lost in your sister that I didn't really notice at the time. Would you allow me to notice now?" he asked.

Her response came with a winning smile, "It appears that after all these years I may have made a good investment."

Allen suddenly had the desire to play the piano that sat on a small stage across the café. He grabbed Ellen's hand and led her across the room. As he sat on the bench she leaned into the bend of the baby grand. Allen began to play "The First Time Ever I Saw Your Face."

"That one was for you," he stated. "This one is for us both." He began playing "You're Nobody 'Til Somebody Loves You."

Ellen blushed as she listened to every note and watched him as he seemed to make every note resound just for her.

Ellen, giggling, sat beside him on the bench and asked, "What was your favorite song when you lived in Austria?"

Switching to the slower melody, Allen said, "When I was sad I loved to play 'Edelweiss.'" As he played the song Ellen smiled at him, but the beauty of the notes soon brought tears to her eyes.

"Now! Now!

"Enough of that," he whispered to her as he switched to a lively rendition of "Love Makes the World Go Round."

By now there were several others who had gathered around the piano in the early morning hour, but Allen's attention was only on Ellen as he began to play, *"It was fascination – I know....Just a passing glance,.... just a brief romance,... and I might have gone empty hearted."*

Allen's heart was filled for the first time in many years as he continued, *"Seeing you alone,....with the moonlight above,....I touched your hand and the next moment I kissed you....Fascination turned to love."* He rose from the bench and took her hand as they walked back to their booth. She moved in and he sat down next to her still holding her hand.

"I wondered if you knew any other songs besides your classical music."

"I enjoy all types of music. I first learned to play Southern Gospel songs and the hymns at church. I didn't read music at the time, but played by ear. I only learned to sight read when I was taught by Professor Karl Brendel, a piano master, in Vienna. That's when I began to practice and play the various methods of classical music."

"You really know how to bring the romance out in the songs you play. In fact, I wanted to kiss you several times while you played just now," she quietly whispered.

Without another word, their eyes met and they leaned toward each other for their first kiss. It was gentle upon their lips, but sparks seemed to ignite as the distance between them was closed.

With deep emotion Ellen said "I have waited for years for that kiss." Allen kissed the single tear that slid down her cheek.

As the sun came up on the two, they drove home tired, but glad that they had spent the night together at the cafe. Before Allen got out of her car he asked, "May I see you again?"

Ellen rolled her eyes at him, "Need you ask?"

"I guess at our age we don't have to be coy with each other," he laughed as he closed the door. He waved as she pulled away and turned around to find Ling standing in the doorway with an all-knowing smirk on his face.

"Don't let me have it yet, Ling. I need to sleep first."

Finally Lasting Love Appears

After weeks of dating Allen and Ellen knew God's call on their lives was still the same as it had been in the past. God had remained faithful to them with His promises and the first to be fulfilled was uniting the two in marriage.

The wedding ceremony was held at the Pleasant Grove church in Greenbrier where Allen had made his original commitment to Christ. Ling, his trusted friend, was his best man, and a fellow associate of Ellen's stood beside her as maid of honor.

The service was simple, but powerful. There was a host of family and friends present to join in the celebration. Ellen's parents had reached their reward, but she knew they would have been overjoyed to see her finally uniting with God's chosen.

David and Martha Livingston were found to be weeping with joy throughout the day. They finally had their son home, and they were gaining a daughter-in-law that they had also fallen in love with.

While they dated Allen and Ellen had shared many conversations about the future left before them. They were in awe as to how God was working out their future together by bringing them both full circle around to the original calling He had placed on their lives.

They approached Mr. and Mrs. Livingston with their final decisions. "Mom, Dad, Ellen and I have decided on the place we want to settle down."

"Oh, is it that new house on Dale Drive?" his mother asked hopefully.

"No, Mom, I'm afraid it's a little farther away than that," Allen answered slowly.

His mother's joy slowly faded as she realized the tone of his voice meant he was getting ready to deliver some hard to accept news. She remembered he had used that very tone on the day he told her and his father that he had joined the Air Force.

"Where?" she managed to asked.

"Laos." The one word hung in the air like a fog.

"You just came home only months ago," pleaded his mother. "You can't possibly leave again so soon. Your father and I are getting old and our time is short."

Allen and Ellen's decision had been made with a God-given peace, and Allen continued without waiving.

"I have shared enough about Friendship Mission that you know where my heart actually is. God originally called me into the ministry, and I now know that He wants me to fulfill His calling at the Mission."

"What about Ellen? You can't possibly think it okay to drag your new bride into that country," countered his mother.

Ellen smiled and placed a hand on Allen's arm to gain control of the conversation. "Mother Livingston, I will not be forced to go. God will also be fulfilling His calling in my life by sending us to Friendship Mission." Ellen took a few minutes to share with Mr. and Mrs. Livingston about her desire to be a medical missionary in a distant or tropical area.

"God will make things pleasant for all of us, Mom. I have faith that He will. My life has been one of often running ahead of or away from God, and now I sincerely believe this is what He wants us to do with our life. I'm going to fully obey Him this time."

David Livingston spoke for the first time. He addressed his wife, "If it is God's will we need to let it alone. If it is not, the plan will come to naught."

"Oh, I know you are both right. I'm just being selfish. Give me a while to accept it, and I will be fine." She admitted as she hugged her two children.

"Thanks, Mom. And now, Ling, will you be going back to Laos with us, or have you decided you like the American way of life?" Allen teased.

"I will begin packing today," Ling replied.

Plans to return to Friendship Mission were well underway. The joy of returning was evident in Allen and Ling and became contagious to the rest of the family. Ling had contacted Princess Ping and she was getting them visas to return to their Asian country.

While Allen and his parents knew they would probably never see each other on this earth again, the Lord had given them all peace and they were in agreement over the departure.

The flight took nearly two full days and the excitement wore their bodies to exhaustion, but stepping foot on the Laos soil and breathing in the new air rejuvenated them.

They were quite surprised when they were met by an envoy from the palace. They were appreciative of the security that was to eventually take them to the compound, but learned they would be stopping at the palace for a welcoming reception provided by the Princess.

As the cars stopped at the entrance, the guards stood in a protected stance as the driver opened the doors for the three guests to walk into the foyer of the old and ornate palace. Allen viewed the surrounding area, but soon focused on the lady sitting on the throne amidst the attendants.

Princess Ping rose to her feet and walked toward Allen, Ellen, and Ling. They bowed before her, and being in front of her servants, she resisted the urge to laugh. Instead, she formally acknowledged their presence and invited them to stand. She then dismissed her servants for a period of private time with her guests.

"Ling, you are looking well. I understand you now have a Master's Degree in Nursing. Congratulations," Ping said as she hugged him.

"Yes, I completed my work while we lived in Vienna," he replied. "And you also are looking fine. I understand you are a mother with two sons."

"Yes, they look much like their father. I spend as much time with them as I can. They are so loving and kind." Ping then turned to Allen, "Is this beautiful woman your wife? I know you are very happy. Ten years have brought changes to all of us, haven't they?"

Allen knew she was being gracious and polite, which was the type lady she had always been, but he could still sense her feelings even though it was hidden behind her words. And yet he knew she was faithful to every word she said.

"We are so happy you have chosen to come back to our country and help our poor and uneducated. I will do all I can to provide any assistance should you need it."

"Thank you, Princess," Allen replied. "We will be highly honored to know you are forever our friend. You have helped us many times over the years, and I want to extend to you my gratitude for each of them," he continued.

"You and Ling have always been close to me, and I know that Ellen will become my friend as well." The genuine sincerity in Ping's voice touched Allen greatly. "I know you are anxious to get to Friendship Mission, but you are welcome here anytime."

Before the Princess was seated the servants entered and prepared for the guests' departure. Soon the cars were loaded and headed for the clinic and compound.

The Desired Finish

Dr. Malin's hair was snow white now and his face wrinkled from time. He was only able to walk with assistance. He started toward Allen slowly with the aid of Song Soo, his trusted assistant. She had been the head nurse in the clinic for as long as Allen had been gone and was now the private caregiver to Dr. Malin.

The moment came for the embrace they had both been longing for. Knowing Dr. Malin was frail; Allen slowly wrapped his arms around his dear, old friend and placed his face next to his. The two held tightly for several minutes.

After many tears and hugging, Dr. Malin said, "I thought I would never see you again, but God has been so good to me. Welcome back Colonel Livingston. Or shall I call you Paul Rasmussen? Perhaps you would like Karl Beetschuzart?" he teased.

"I would like nothing better than to be called 'my boy' again," admitted Allen.

With a fresh round of tears, Dr. Malin patted Allen's cheek with his aged hand. "Oh, my boy, I am so proud of you. Thank you for returning to this old man. And now tell me who this beautiful, young woman is."

"Dr. Malin Rasmussen, I want you to meet my wife, Dr. Ellen Livingston."

Malin slowly hugged Ellen and questioned, "You are a doctor? My wife was a doctor too. She brought me here to start this mission, and now I have spent nearly all my life here helping the infirmed and poor. My wife was a godly lady, beautiful and kind. She lives up on that hill now, but I visit her every day. She was always concerned as to who would follow us here and take over our work." In the middle of his musings, Dr. Malin's eyes suddenly lit up as if a revelation had come to him. He choked on a sob as he quietly ventured, "Dr. Ellen, has God sent you here?"

"Yes sir, He has," she humbly answered.

Dr. Malin placed a hand over his heart and looking up to the heavens silently thanked the Lord. "Allen, come take this old man to the chapel. There are many there waiting to see you and Ling again."

After an initial hello to everyone, Dr. Malin had everyone take a seat. Li Snoog marched to the piano and began to play "I'll Meet You by the River Some Sweet Day." This was one of Allen's favorites and he remembered singing it often with Dr. Malin as they walked to and from the cemetery in the evenings.

Dr. Malin stood and after giving thanks for the traveling mercies, to the shock of those seated, began to give his last will and testament.

"I've never been one who allowed closeness with many. There is one, nearly forty years younger than me, that sits here today as my friend, brother, and fellow laborer.

"We had opportunity to spend much time together in Allen's last years here. We bonded most during our walks together. I remember how he was so overwhelmed by the beauty of this area. It never failed on any of our walks up the hill that he wouldn't exclaim, 'I just can't believe it!' He may just now be saying those very same words for a different reason.

"I turned eighty years old last week and in a few days my death will change everything. In a few days I will depart to bask in the sunlight of Heaven. I am ready to walk on golden streets, to gaze upon the inexpressible glories that will surround me forever! Thank you, Allen, for helping me to be sure about my destiny.

"Now, I have written what I want carved on my stone. Allen, come here and read what this says while I sit for a moment."

Allen took the handwritten message from Dr. Malin, but he

wasn't sure that he could read around the lump in his throat.

"Go ahead, my boy. Read it for everyone to hear," Dr. Malin encouraged.

Allen began reading his friend's last words of encouragement to the compound.

It is not for us to ask "WHY?" but rather "WHEN?"
Since each of us will depart so prepare for "THEN."
The Question is "WHERE" is our spirit going
With full assurance in Christ – Knowing.
For Life exists in the Father's Son
And only in Him is earth's victory won.
Our beloved Lord who still lives today,
Preached of the end, with the power to sway.
He never promoted the "WHY" but preached about "WHEN"
So all of His followers would go "THERE" when it came to "THEN."

With Allen's assistance, Dr. Malin stood once again and motioned for Ellen to join them. He looked into the younger faces and asked, "Will you accept the work that Dr. Angelika and I began here over fifty years ago?"

Both Allen and Ellen knew God wanted them to continue the work there. They shook their heads and Dr. Malin shouted to those seated, "Friendship Mission, I give you Allen and Dr. Ellen. They will take good care of you."

Dr. Malin, who had the utmost respect for Ling, turned to him next and said, "You know more about running everything on the compound than most anyone here. Can I count on you to keep Allen in line?"

Ling assured Dr. Malin that he would do his best.

"Good! Good!" announced Dr. Malin. "And now I must rest. Song Soo?" he summoned. Song Soo graciously helped Dr. Malin back to his room and made him comfortable. Upon returning to the chapel she found that everyone had left except Allen, Ellen, and Ling. They had just finished praying at the altar. Song Soo decided to remain in the back so as not to interrupt.

Allen hugged Ling. "Ellen and I will be so glad to have you here at the compound with us. We know your heart is as attached to the ministry as ours. You and Song Soo can help Ellen care for the clinic and I will speak in the chapel and teach the interested," he announced.

With his last statement came a gentle sob from the back of the chapel. The three turned to find Song Soo standing with a look of relief on her face. "Can I really continue my work here? I have no other home but this one."

Ling started toward Song Soo and embraced her. "You will always have a home here with me," he assured her.

Two days later, as he predicted, the aged doctor passed into eternity. Dr. Malin Rasmussen was buried beside his wife, Dr. Angelika Mowrer Rasmussen and their four children in a land where they served more than fifty years.

It was the request of Dr. Malin that no flowery sermon or committal be said over him, so Allen said only one thing. "Someone once told me, 'A friend is a person to whom you do not have to explain anything.' Dr. Malin was one for me. Few have ever met with such a loss – for few have ever had such a friend to lose. I did."

Allen and Dr. Ellen Livingston and Ling and Song Soo Kai fulfilled the wish of Dr. Angelika Rasmussen: "Who will follow us?"

There Will Be Someone to Follow Us

www.ingramcontent.com/pod-product-compliance
Lightning Source LLC
Chambersburg PA
CBHW070953040426
42443CB00007B/489